Printed in the United States of America

Paperback ISBN: 978-0-9862983-5-6

Cover/Interior Design by Creative Artistic Excellence
https://creativeartisticexcellence.com

Please Fire Me! I Can't Stand My Boss

How Today's Leaders Build Relationships,
Job Satisfaction, & Retention

By Bella Cruz

Dedication

To my children Rene, Jonathan, and Sarah, and all my grandchildren throughout the generations. Your purpose was given to you when God Almighty created you. Use it to help others, and live your life with passion!

Table of Contents

Foreword

My last 30 years as a lifestyle entrepreneur traveling the globe, working on red carpets, and holding records in television network news, as well as my appearances, have connected with me an incredible array of thought leaders, entrepreneurs, and mentors.

I first started to work with Bella Cruz during the time that she was nominated for the *Women of Heart Awards* and received the *International Author and Global Leadership Award* from London, England, UK. As the executive producer and brand mentor of the *Women of Heart Awards*, I have the unique privilege and access to many amazing leaders around the world. It was rare to find such a jewel in my backyard and to discover that Bella and I shared hometown origins, favorite local spots, and similar philosophies. It has been my honor to work with Bella, first as a mentor and now as a dear friend.

When I first heard the main title of Bella's book, *Please Fire Me! I Can't Stand my Boss*, I was inspired to learn more about those who are so unhappy with their jobs that they wish to be fired by their bosses. Reading further, I discovered refreshing, humorous, and cringe-worthy facts about how bosses, supervisors, and leaders who intentionally and unintendedly treat those under their care. Her subtitle, *How Today's Leaders Build Relationships, Job Satisfaction, & Retention* is a preview of a book full of smart and effective stories, strategies, and tactical tips that every leader should know.

I was embarrassed to see some of the examples and mistakes that I had made over the years as a young entrepreneur while attempting to mentor, lead, nurture, and manage teams. I started at age 23 and sometimes managed my team more like a family than an entrepreneur. When providing training to my teams, I didn't see that I had displayed aspects of the *"Read My Mind Leader"* found under Principle 5, *Tell Me What Accountability Looks Like...* Wow! What a gut punch for my ego, since I prided myself on fairness in training. No matter our current levels of success, we can always learn every single day how to be a better leader.

You will learn tips, lessons, and strategies that help managers and supervisors empower individuals to increase job satisfaction and achieve greater levels of productivity and profits. You will learn how to be the leader who takes your employees on a journey to build more leaders!

Reading *Please Fire Me! I Can't Stand My Boss* is an enlightening, humorous, and educational experience. It will point you to the areas of your leadership skills that are producing win-win results and show you how you can correct the areas where you may be falling short, which can affect your career as a leader as well as the employees in your trusted care. It is so helpful that, throughout this book, Bella has provided questions designed to help you assess your leadership style to self-diagnose where you are exceling and where you can improve to build your team(s). When you answer these questions that help you take an active role in developing your leadership skills, you will continue your journey of excellence.

I can see the focus and care that Bella has put into this career-changing book and how she pulls from her discipline as a certified Six Sigma Black Belt. Bella definitely walks her talk and has the credentials to back it up, not only with her master's degree and the status of an Amazon #1 Bestselling Author, but also from her 25 years in the corporate world as a leadership strategist and coach working with CEOs, leaders, and supervisors around the world.

Thank you, Bella Cruz, global speaker and international bestselling author of *Please Fire Me! I Can't Stand My Boss,* which reveals *How Today's Leaders Build Relationships, Job Satisfaction, & Retention.*

With love, respect, and admiration from your mentor, colleague, student, and friend,

Starley Murray
Celebrity Lifestyle Entrepreneur
CEO of Lifestyle TV News

Introduction

During a meeting with some HR executives many years ago, a loud exclamation made everyone in the room jump: "Please! Please fire me!" An employee was screaming just outside the door with desperation in her voice. "I can't stand my boss! It's *torture* coming to work every day!"

Her words struck right to my core — not just because of her shocking outburst, and not even because I had already spoken to many like her throughout my coaching career. I got chills because, at one point, I *was* her. I felt her pain, and I knew it all too well.

Before launching my coaching business, I had worked for a boss who made work an absolute nightmare. This supervisor wasn't the kind of absent leader that leaves you to your own devices, although that kind of leader can also sap the atmosphere out of a workplace. No — instead, this leader actively worked against me. He twisted my words, sabotaged my work, and portrayed me to others as hopelessly incompetent.

I could barely look at my supervisor without nausea setting in because of the stress he caused me, and I would lie awake at night wondering how he would try to betray me the next day.

To make things even worse, my coworkers also took up arms against me. I was excluded from team activities, kept out of meetings, and left out of important emails; they also spoke to me with a condescending voice. John Maxwell says that everything rises and falls on leadership. A leader sets the tone for his and her followers, and this leader's tone was openly hostile toward me, so everyone else's was too.

With my supervisor and my coworkers working against me, I was destined to fail. You can't win a war on two fronts, especially one in which you don't even know why you're fighting. I could barely get anything done, and believe it or not, neither could anyone else. I had become such a big target that most of the team was no longer pursuing the company's strategic goals as a priority. Most of the employees were focusing on the supervisor's primary goal of getting me fired.

Finally, I got so fed up that I quit… and I used my experience as a model of what *not* to do when leading. I made it my mission to bridge the gap between employees and supervisors — to learn how they best work together, boil it down to a science, and help cultivate an emotionally and financially thriving culture in every business that hired me.

Since then, I have conducted thousands of workshops, surveys, and face-to-face interviews. I have spoken to hundreds of thousands of employees and supervisors on every imaginable rung of the corporate leadership ladder. I have seen businesses in many industries transform their turnover rate, engagement, efficiency, productivity, customer satisfaction, and ultimately, their bottom line. And what made the difference for them?

Trust & Accountability!

In my 25-year corporate leadership coaching and speaking career, the two areas where companies needed the most help — and that were most vital to their success — were, and are, trust and accountability. Many workplaces suffer from a huge divide between the supervisors and the employees — a divide that easily allows doubt, assumptions, and fear to fill in. Everything rises and falls on leadership, and for better or for worse, the leader is responsible for his or her team. It is up to the leader to bridge that gap. And leaders can only bridge it when they hold themselves accountable and prove themselves trustworthy to their employees.

In *Please Fire Me! I Can't Stand My Boss,* I have outlined the same seven principles of leadership that have helped me help corporations turn around their culture and their revenue, with the practical dos and don'ts that bring those principles to life. I have also included my signature *Accountability Performance Model* © in the book for your reference, or for you to use as a guide when creating your own. Implement the insights in this book, and you can create a high-trust accountability culture in your workplace.

NOTE: All of the stories in this book are true. They are drawn from my experience working with various companies as a leadership corporate strategist. To protect the identities of the parties involved, all proper names of companies, locations, and individuals have been changed.

Principle 1
Have Integrity

Sophia's Legacy

Sophia Alexander was one of the most effective leaders I worked with in my career as an executive coach. Sophia was an executive with more than 30 years' experience working for a company with several locations around the globe. In that time, she had cultivated a reputation that preceded her. Before I even met her, I had seen the impact that her integrity and competence had on her peers, her employees, the customers, the vendors, and even the greater community. She was known for her innovative problem-solving and great communication skills, and she had the lowest turnover rate in the company to show for it.

One day, as I was walking through the halls of this company, I saw what looked like the start of Sophia's team meeting. The conference room was neatly arranged with tables, chairs, and a large screen. Each employee had come prepared to take notes, and none of them had a phone out. This team was clearly expecting a productive discussion. They were relaxed, and even actively engaged. They talked, smiled, and laughed with each other as they waited for the meeting to start. It wasn't awkward or tense; it was comfortable and professional. Sophia was definitely doing something right! When I saw her at the front of the room, I asked if I could sit in to observe, and she said yes.

I have attended so many meetings that they tend to blend together in my memory. Most meetings are not grounded by an agenda, and the employees scroll on their phones or stare blankly ahead until they're called upon. None of that was going on in Sophia's meeting.

The meeting began on time, and in the first thirty seconds, each teammate had an agenda, someone was assigned to take notes, and the meeting's talking points were projected on the screen at the front of the room.

Everyone could see all the team projects, who was accountable for each project, the deadlines, and the metrics for measuring the results.

Sophia facilitated the meeting with precision. She addressed each teammate directly, asking specific *Team Performance Questions* such as:

1) What went well with your job this week?
2) What did not go well?
3) Where did you get stuck?

Accountable leaders use open-ended questions like these to draw out important details from their employees, and then they use those insights to lead their teams more effectively to improve performance, enhance communication, and solve problems.

As the meeting continued, the team members took turns like clockwork, answering each of these questions thoughtfully and confidently. Not only were they knowledgeable about their assignments, but they also trusted Sophia implicitly. If something didn't go right with their projects, they weren't afraid to tell the group. They didn't have to keep silent for fear of looking incompetent or being punished. Why? Because that wasn't the culture in this department.

As the meeting came to a close, the subject turned to Sophia. After her long, illustrious career, she would be retiring soon, and the team's appreciation of her was evident. Everyone went on about how much they would miss her. Someone even admitted that he would "take a bullet" for her. The rest of Sophia's team laughed, but they all nodded in agreement. Whatever Sophia had done for them, they were all willing to catch bullets on her behalf. Of course, this was only an expression, but it spoke volumes about her leadership style.

Once the meeting was over, I asked Sophia if I could learn more about how she led her team. "Your team loves you, and they love working here," I said. "You just can't fake that behavior. To what do you attribute this incredible leadership win?"

She replied, "When we win, we do it together." She spoke about her team with great sincerity and pride.

"If we fail, I have to be the first to accept accountability. I consider failure an opportunity to shift gears and get the team back on the right track. This attitude has helped my employees feel comfortable asking for help when they need it. They are committed to the team, the organization's strategic goals, and their results have created great success for this company. The leader's attitude has such an impact on the team, and of course, the team directly impacts results."

Sophia practiced many of the high-trust accountability behaviors outlined in this book. If you follow her example, your team can pull together to help your organization meet its loftiest goals.

"High-performance teams thrive with high-trust, accountable leaders."

~ Bella Cruz

Principle 1
Have Integrity

The Dos

1) DO create trust with others

One company I worked with was being audited as part of its annual inspections. When one department's compliance was called into question, the executive in the room started asking questions, including whether that department was compliant. Everyone said yes.

The executive then turned to one of the directors in the room and asked him directly, "Are they compliant? I know you will tell me the truth and not just what I want to hear." The room went silent.

Most people don't get put on the spot like this in meetings. However, the point of this story is that everyone has a reputation. Your history follows you into every situation because you create a public impression of yourself every time you take action with others. When your actions give people a reason to trust you, they trust you, and when they trust you, you will be able to lead them much more effectively. People want to follow an accountable leader with a track record of overcoming challenges with integrity and competence.

> "A leader's most powerful ally is his or her own example. Leaders don't just talk about doing something; they do it."
>
> ~ John Wooden

2) DO be honest

Honest leaders tell the truth. If they make a mistake, they are the first to admit it, and they do whatever they can to make it right. These leaders serve as an example; they communicate with their actions that honesty is an important value to the company. They model honesty for their employees and expect honesty from them in return. This naturally develops a high-trust culture of accountability in the workplace.

> "Honesty is a key characteristic of a business because it sets the tone for the kind of work culture that you want to create, provides consistency in workplace behavior, and builds loyalty and trust in customers and prospects."[1]

3) DO respect everyone

Respect is foundational to integrity. No one wants to work with or hang around with people who don't respect them. Disrespect might look like promoting yourself and not others, not giving others credit for their contributions, holding yourself and others to different standards, or treating someone unfairly because of his or her job or position.

"In an HBR study of nearly 20,000 employees, half of those don't feel respected by their bosses. Respectful leadership means treating everyone regardless of rank, status, or position, with the same genuine regard and consideration you would like them to give you… When employees feel genuinely respected by their boss, they are more likely to work hard, stay loyal, and go the extra mile when the going gets rough."[2]

Someone who has integrity gives respect first. Respectful, integrous leaders know their team's capabilities and promote teamwork. When they are speaking to others, they listen without interrupting or dominating the conversation. They respect the privacy of their employees and ensure that they are providing their team with a dignified, collaborative workspace. These leaders make decisions based on what's right, not based on employee personalities or "personal favorites."

When employees feel like you're respecting their time and their jobs, you will get their commitment when it comes to making team decisions. As with honesty, respectful leaders set the tone for the office atmosphere and surround themselves with people who prioritize respect. In meetings, people will be engaged with you instead of with their technology; when you acknowledge them, they will acknowledge you.

Everyone wants to work with a supervisor who respects and cares about them. If you become an intentional leader who respects and appreciates the diversity of and contributions from each member of your team, they will help you meet the strategic goals of your company.

> "The supreme quality for leadership is unquestionably integrity. Without it, no real success is possible, no matter whether it is on a section gang, a football field, in an army, or in an office."
>
> ~ Dwight D. Eisenhower

4) **DO** keep your promises

Over and over again in workshops, I hear stories from employees about supervisors who promise awards, luncheons, bonuses, and celebrations for jobs well done; but some never become a reality. When this topic comes up, employees often get emotional.

On the other hand, when I've conducted leadership masterminds and workshops, supervisors admit that they do appreciate their employees and want to celebrate them — but they're busy. Time passes, and before you know it, they've broken their promise to their employees, which affects team dynamics.

It's important to be accountable. Do what you say you're going to do and be on time with your commitments. If you cannot do something, keep the team members updated and tell them why you can't do it. When you keep your promises, your credibility goes up, and you start building solid relationships of high-trust. The foundation of every relationship is trust, and when it's gone, everyone knows it.

"Trust is like the air we breathe — when it's present, nobody really notices; when it's absent, everybody notices."

~ Warren Buffett

5) DO be dependable

Having integrity includes being dependable. When leaders are dependable, they show up! They are reliable, and the team can depend on them to consistently support them and keep them informed. They also keep their commitments to the team, their projects, and the organization. When you are reliable, it helps you earn credibility, foster trust, and sustain a culture of integrity.

6) DO hold yourself accountable

It is easy for some leaders to want to appear as though their judgment is perfect, and sometimes they might even avoid owning up to their mistakes. But teams cannot grow in any substantial way when the leader isn't holding himself or herself accountable first. Leaders lead by example. Blame-throwing leaders create blame-throwing cultures, and accountable leaders create accountable cultures.

Accountable leaders take responsibility for the successes and failures of the team and its projects. They recognize their role in — and responsibility for — developing the team. If a team member fails, the leader is ultimately responsible, and he or she should be proactive in developing the expectations, goals, resources, and support that the team needs to succeed.

When leaders admit to their mistakes and take ownership of them, they can fix the problems and move past them more quickly. This inspires the same accountability from the team. They feel empowered to ask for important resources and information. Ultimately, the team performs better, and the company gains a competitive edge.

People learn by watching others, and how you hold yourself and the team accountable determines whether or not the team trusts you to lead.

7) **DO** have courage

Good supervisors stand tall against adversity that works against them or their teams; they support their teams and provide them with resources. Leaders demonstrate integrity when they dare to do the right thing, especially when it's not popular! It takes courage to own your mistakes, to defend your team when it makes mistakes, to face problems head-on, and to address team conflict promptly.

Being a leader is not always easy, but courage will help you become the leader your team needs you to be. By courageously implementing all the principles in this book, you can create for yourself a reputation of integrity and earn the loyalty and engagement of your team.

> "The courage of leadership is giving others a chance to succeed even though you bear the responsibility for getting things done."
> ~ Simon Sinek

Throughout this book, you will find questions designed to help you assess your leadership style in order to self-diagnose where you are exceling and where you can improve to build your team(s). I encourage you to take the time to answer these questions to help you take an active role in developing your leadership skills to continue your journey of excellence.

Leadership Questions

1) Describe the integrity characteristics you show your team to create trust in the workplace.

_____

_____

_____

2) How do you show respect to everyone on your team?

_____

_____

_____

Principle 1
Have Integrity

The "No Courage" Leader

Colin Green sat fidgeting at the front of the conference room. Colin was the director of a ten-person team, and the company he worked for had brought me in to coach him. On this particular day, it was hard to watch him awkwardly avoid eye contact with his team. They were eagerly awaiting the start of the meeting, and they whispered among themselves in anticipation. But Colin was stalling as long as he could. He was about to let down his team, and, as I would find out later, in more ways than one.

This company had hired me because Colin's team was falling behind. They were working on several projects, but they often performed poorly and missed deadlines. After I started working with them, it became very clear why: during the workday, it was common to see employees visiting with each other, laughing, and carrying on about personal things. Some employees even made it a habit of coming in late or leaving early. Colin wanted to be liked, so he had a hard time holding people accountable.

Then, Colin's team was assigned a major time-sensitive project. The department's executive director came in to discuss specifics and expectations, and with this injection of accountability, the entire team dynamic changed. They became engaged. They were active and invested, and they started producing with real traction.

But not long into their new flow, they hit a roadblock. A problem with other departments and external suppliers kept them from moving forward with the project. Colin knew he couldn't solve this problem himself and would have to ask his boss for help. But he wouldn't do that. He was too afraid of looking incompetent in front of his boss, and he was intimidated by her title. He didn't want to have the conversation, so he put it off, and put it off, and put it off. His team grew frustrated. The productive energy that the department director brought with her had faded, and the project deadline was fast approaching.

Finally, Colin told the team that he would meet with his boss. Knowing they would soon be making progress, Colin's team got excited, and you could feel the energy in the room change.

Then, the day came... the day that Colin sat fidgeting in front of his team in the conference room, dodging their eager eyes. He began the meeting with a dry, flat, "I met with my boss." Everyone leaned forward. "She's too busy to help right now." The room completely deflated. Colin's team members sat back in their chairs, scoffing quietly. Even I felt my heart sink a little.

But that disappointment quickly became shocking when I caught up with Colin's executive department director. When I asked her about the project and her meeting with Colin, she gave me a puzzled look. "What meeting?" she asked.

"When Colin asked you to help his team with its project," I clarified.

"He never asked me for help on any project." And, in fact, he hadn't. Colin had not just disappointed his team; he had lied to them too. He couldn't hold himself accountable to them.

Courageous leaders take risks and make changes to increase profits, retention, and drive strategic focus. Proactively affecting your organization is an integral function of leadership, and you will need courage to have the difficult conversations that bring lasting change.

In return, your team will not only respect you, but they will also stand by you through success and failure alike.

"Courage combined with integrity is the foundation of character."

~ Brian Tracy

Principle 1
Have Integrity

The Don'ts

1) **DON'T** tell lies

"According to research, people most want their leaders to be honest… Honesty is selected more often than any other leadership characteristic. For people to willingly follow someone, they first want to assure themselves that the individual has integrity and is worthy of their trust."[3]

Even "little white lies" undermine trust. One employee said in one of my workshops that her supervisor's favorite line was, "A little white lie won't hurt anyone! How many of you haven't told a little white lie?" I asked the class what they thought about someone who says things like that, and the responses all came down to one answer: They wouldn't trust that supervisor!

> "[In a] recent study by the Harvard Business Review… [r]esearchers found that if they could get people to cheat a little the first time, they'd be willing to cheat a bit more the second time, and finally cheat "big" the third time."[4]

2) DON'T make promises you won't keep

It's simple… Don't make promises that you know are out of your control, or that you just won't keep. Your employees remember when you don't keep your promises.

> "People with good intentions make promises, but people with good character keep them."
> ~ Anonymous

3) DON'T do anything illegal

Yes, it seems obvious when it's written down in plain ink. But sadly, in my career, I have heard of leaders breaking the law, or at least trying to do it.

During one of my coaching sessions, one employee told me that her boss had asked her to change the numbers on a report to make the department look good. The employee refused to do it, and she said she couldn't believe that her boss asked her to change the report data. She said to me, "I lost all respect for my supervisor that day!"

Some people will do whatever it takes to hold onto power, to look good in front of others, or to be recognized with awards. In the workplace, some employees will look the other way when they see their leader doing something illegal; most will report it, but others will follow his or her lead. However, most will lose respect and trust in their leaders when they see this behavior. Leaders need to be intentional about the use of their power — not abusing it, but instead using it wisely to help others.

"We are free to choose our actions… but we are not free to choose the consequences of these actions."

~ Stephen R. Covey

4) DON'T take shortcuts

Taking shortcuts might happen for many reasons such as tight deadlines, meeting quotas, working with non-compliant equipment, working on multiple projects, being short-staffed, and job complacency. Taking shortcuts may seem more efficient at the time, but shortcuts can cause serious safety issues, and even deadly consequences.

"Taking shortcuts on the job is a sign of poor SafetyDNA™. Employees are statistically six times more likely to experience an accident or injury as a result of unsafe behaviors, such as taking shortcuts… One large insurance firm even reported that 92% of their reported injury and workers' compensation claims occurred because workers were not performing their tasks properly."[5]

Supervisors should educate their teams often on the risks and consequences of taking shortcuts, encourage following all precautions and guidelines, and reward those who perform and comply with the company's safety standards.

Leadership Questions

1) How do you prevent breaking promises to your team?

_____

_____

_____

2) How do you handle situations (demonstrate courage) when you have to make difficult decisions?

_____

_____

_____

Principle 2
Be Competent

The Team Roars for George

Have you ever seen an audience get so excited that they got up out of their seats and cheered *at a work function in front of hundreds of people?* This kind of display is not common in today's corporate world. But George Long's team was so excited to work with him that they just couldn't hold it in.

George Long was an executive director at a Fortune 500 company whose business model was changing. The company was growing; new revenue opportunities were waiting to be claimed; and a new competitive position in the market was open for the taking. But in order to excel, it had to expand. This company hired a number of consulting experts — myself included — to guide the transition to success with strategic planning sessions.

This company's leadership team was intentional through every step of the planning process. They crafted teams with members from diverse backgrounds and areas of expertise, carefully selecting which executive director would lead each team. They modeled competence from the top down.

Once the strategic plan was ready to execute, a huge company-wide meeting was held to mark the occasion. Hundreds of employees, supervisors, and executive directors were in attendance, all of them neatly dressed and pressed. The CEO welcomed everyone with a ceremonial speech, and a presentation was given that communicated project expectations. Then, the time came for the executive leader to announce to each team who their team leader would be for the project.

As each name was called, the executive director would leave his or her seat and join the chosen team. Every director was met with cordial smiles and firm handshakes…

…except George Long.

When George's team members heard his name called, they all stood up from their seats and *roared!* They filled the whole auditorium with their cheers and wild applause, high-fiving and carrying on like they were at a rock concert. Every eye was on them. George approached his team with confidence, humility, and gratitude.

No one had been expecting such a red-carpet welcome for a team leader. It wasn't that the other team leaders were ineffective; this company was very discerning, and it had put its teams in good hands. But George's team had welcomed him so explosively because they *knew* he was competent and *cared* about people! George was one of those leaders who really knew how to connect with people to make them feel like they mattered and contributed to the team. He respected them and valued their input. He knew his job, did it, and actively engaged his employees. His team was so excited because George had earned his incredible reputation, and its members knew that their project would yield great results under his leadership because he was competent consistently!

When you demonstrate competence in a way that uplifts others, they will be your greatest advocates. They will sing your praises louder than you ever could.

> "Employees don't want to work for a manager that just delegates; they want to work for a leader who takes them on a journey of success!"
>
> ~ Bella Cruz

Principle 2
Be Competent

The Dos

1) DO communicate often with employees

Communication is not supposed to replicate a racquetball game, where one person at a time hits the ball against the wall. This is like one person doing all the talking during a conversation. Effective communication is like playing tennis, where you take turns communicating back and forth when you're talking to each other.

A high-performing team is always communicating with each other. They communicate face-to-face or through technology, and they have systems in place to communicate with everyone promptly.

A competent leader intentionally schedules time to make leadership rounds and holds one-on-one meetings with the individuals on their teams, while keeping everyone informed in the workplace. Not only do they communicate often, but they are intentional about being in the moment while communicating with others. They also listen patiently to understand the other person's point of view, instead of waiting for the moment to take over the conversation.

"Most people do not listen with the intent to understand; they listen with the intent to reply."
~ Stephen R. Covey

2) DO stay informed

I've conducted so many leadership workshops with supervisors and managers who didn't even know where their company's organizational chart was located. Some leaders couldn't tell me what their company's mission or vision was, or how their department fit into the company's bigger strategic goals.

Some supervisors keep making decisions that cause repetitive work or cost the company profits because they don't know their company's policies or how to lead their teams. Knowing your job and knowing more about your organization will help you make decisions that best serve your team and your company. This is especially important if you are a new supervisor in the organization or department!

Stay informed by learning about your company, its mission, vision, organizational chart, culture, projects, policies, budgets, employee recognition awards, and anything else that could contribute to the team's success. A competent leader learns all of these things. You can also stay informed, and make your company gain a competitive edge in the marketplace by researching best practices. Competence includes knowing who the individuals are on your team and how they can best contribute with their particular skills and talents.

Accountability is always top-down. Knowing your job helps you make the right decisions and accelerates team performance.

"Leadership is an action, not a position."
~ Donald McGannon

3) DO learn your job and get good at it

One company I worked with created a committee of team members from several different departments to work on a corporate-wide project. When one member was late to a committee meeting, someone said, "We can't depend on that department… it never gets things done! It's like pulling teeth every time we ask it to do something, and no one ever answers emails. I hope they don't show up because it will be a total waste of time having them on the team, and we have to do all their work anyway!"

Our fast-paced, agility-driven world becomes less and less tolerant of delays, mistakes, and incompetence. A leader must replace age-old practices with new technologies, business models, and processes to be considered innovative in business today. In this world, competence is just as important as integrity. You can have great integrity and not be competent at what you do, or you can be great at your job and have no integrity. Both are equally important to create influential leadership!

> "Our research also revealed that 53% of employees who don't trust their managers feel this way because their managers 'don't appear to know what they are doing.'... Inevitably, this creates another opportunity for trust to collapse, dragging job satisfaction and employee retention down with it too."[6]

Understanding and getting good at executing your job simplifies your decision-making, improves your efficiency, and nurtures your confidence as a leader. This also helps you better prepare for your strategic meetings with your teams. Again, leaders lead by example; competent supervisors hire and inspire competent employees; and competent employees exceed customer expectations, which increases customer loyalty, trust, and profits.

4) **DO** use tools for greater outcomes

One important part of being competent is knowing what tools to use to help you amplify your results. There are so many teams that get nowhere with their projects or goals, or that have to start projects over because they had no clear directions to guide their actions. Today, there are lots of apps and user-friendly programs that can help you grow and leverage your business to gain a competitive edge in the marketplace. There are also models with powerful proven successes that can help you if you use them consistently. For example, before delegating projects to your team(s), you can use the SMART goal model as a tool to gain clarity on projects of all sizes and scopes. If you use the tool consistently, the SMART goals model can help you execute the right goals for your projects, create metrics to measure the outcomes, and meet your deadlines to complete the projects successfully.

"SMART is an acronym that you can use to guide your goal setting... To make sure that your goals are clear and reachable, each one should be:

- Specific (simple, sensible, significant)
- Measurable (meaningful, motivating)
- Achievable (agreed, attainable)
- Relevant (reasonable, realistic, and resourced, results-based)
- Time-bound (time-based, time-limited, time/cost limited, timely, time-sensitive)"[7]

Using the SMART goals model and other productivity tools can help you obtain clarity, which helps you to make better decisions, improve your effectiveness, and increase productivity speed.

5) DO write things down and schedule them

How many times have you missed a meeting, a project deadline, or writing a recognition award for an employee because you didn't write it down or put it on your calendar? Writing things down keeps everything organized, action-oriented, and stress-free (or stress-minimized).

> "When we write something down, research suggests that as far as our brain is concerned, it's as if we were doing that thing. Writing seems to act as a kind of mini-rehearsal for doing..."[8]

6) DO execute the project

I remember one executive who was the most charming person you could ever meet. She was a great communicator, and she could convince people to do almost anything she wanted them to do. But she never completed projects; she couldn't produce results. Soon, her charm turned into a reputation of broken promises and incompetence.

High-trust, accountable leaders don't just make commitments; they execute, modify, follow through, and complete projects whose results exceed expectations. And because leaders lead by example, the team is inspired to follow suit. Team output improves as it embraces personal responsibility, which in turn increases profits and business intelligence.

> "The path to success is to take massive, determined actions."
>
> ~ Tony Robbins

Leadership Questions

1) How do you gain the competitive intelligence you
   need to lead your team and the company successfully
   in the marketplace?

   _____

   _____

   _____

2) What tools or programs do you use to make sure that
   you execute your projects successfully and on time?

   _____

   _____

   _____

Principle 2
Be Competent

The "What's Your Title?" Leader

O ne executive I worked with — Lacey King —
had such a social influence that she was
practically the mascot of the company. You
would find her at every single company luncheon, social
event, and executive meeting. You would find her
volunteering for notable local committees. You would
even find her on social media networking with big names
in her industry. Lacey was everywhere, all the time.

And everywhere you found her, she made an
impression. She had a distinct, unique magnetism — a
charming, in-the-moment presence that she carried with

confidence. She had a knack for getting people to talk about their interests, and while they talked, she looked them in the eyes and listened intently. Her body language and dynamic inflection conveyed that she was invested in the conversation. Because she was such a compelling communicator (and so visible, and so involved), Lacey was a standout director who was often selected for high-profile projects.

But despite Lacey's front-facing communication skills, her visibility, and her involvement, she had one of the company's highest turnover rates. Her employees avoided her at all costs and complained about her to anyone who would listen. The Lacey that leadership knew and the Lacey that her employees described were completely different people.

One day, a water main burst in front of Lacey's building. It was like a giant fountain shooting water up from under the ground, and most of her employees had crowded around the windows to watch in awe. Because she was in charge of the building, Lacey was responsible for coordinating with the maintenance supervisor to deal with the situation. But when he stopped her in the hall, she couldn't have appeared more distant. She was closed off — her head down, ignoring him completely, and scrolling through her phone to read her virtual newsfeed. She didn't say a single word to him. No connection. No emotion. No eye contact. No respect for this person or his job. Her magnetism was gone. Where did her charm go? She had left it in the boardroom.

Lacey surrounded herself with people whose positions were higher than hers on the organizational chart, and she had a supernatural ability to work the room. Her charm would even kick in at family gatherings, where she thought there might be someone who could help her further her career. But if you couldn't help her… it was like you didn't exist. It's no mystery why Lacey's high turnover rate and bad team rapport had developed.

Make no mistake: communication and engagement are necessary leadership skills, but an engaging communicator doesn't necessarily make an effective leader. Titles mean little when they are compared to reputation. Leadership qualities must go in *all* directions. Those "above" you, those "below" you, and those "beside" you on the organizational chart all deserve respect. Remember, you are all on the same ship, heading to the same destination.

> "Leadership is not about titles, positions, or flowcharts. It is about one life influencing another."
>
> ~ John C. Maxwell

Principle 2
Be Competent

The Don'ts

1) DON'T judge people based on their titles

Most of us have experienced people changing their tone of voice, their body language, or the attention they give us based on our title. People lose respect for leaders — and sometimes even resent them — when they treat people negatively or insincerely. How you treat your employees affects how they treat their duties, which directly impacts your customers and your company's strategic goals. It takes connecting and caring about people, regardless of their title, to earn their respect and collaboration.

"I've learned that people will forget what you said, people will forget what you did, but people will never forget how you made them feel."

~ Maya Angelou

2) DON'T miss deadlines

So many projects fail, people become disappointed, companies are penalized with late fees, services from vendors are put on hold, and companies lose revenue because projects are not completed on time. And so many of these missed deadlines are the result of absent or disorganized leaders or leaders who don't hold their employees accountable.

Employees want their supervisors to lead by holding themselves accountable first and to hold others accountable as well. They want to work for a competent supervisor who knows how to leverage best practices and helps employees get things done on time.

Be a supervisor who empowers, creates independence, and models personal accountability in the workplace by meeting the deadlines for your projects.

3) DON'T be overconfident

Some leaders might become overconfident because of their title or position, but still perform poorly. Remember, the team can only perform at or below its leader's performance level. If its leader is not performing well, the team doesn't either. This can create not just a toxic workplace environment, but also a miserable one; it is a deadly combination for diminishing morale. Overconfidence is not the same thing as competence.

> "Competent leaders cause high levels of trust, engagement, and productivity, [but] incompetent ones result in anxious, alienated workers who practice counterproductive work behaviors and spread toxicity throughout the firm."[9]

Take the time to learn your job and understand your leadership style. Humility and competence do wonders for your influence on the team.

Leadership Questions

1) What leadership habits do you practice to stay informed and competent at your job?

_____

_____

_____

2) How do you prevent judging someone by his or her title?

_____

_____

_____

Principle 3
Be Approachable

Lighting Up the Room!

Mia Strong's workplace was thriving. Profits were up, turnover was down, her team members loved their jobs, and they loved working with Mia.

The energy changed when Mia walked into the room and people lit up like Christmas trees! They would trip over each other to talk to her, getting up from their desks or out of their cubicles; even managers would come out of their offices to catch up with her.

Why? What was the reason behind such success and charisma?

Mia made herself the most approachable person in the company. Mia was competent in her duties, but she also went beyond just competence; she ensured that all of her employees and colleagues knew her to be sincere, with good intentions. She helped others without expecting anything for herself; she was intentional about communicating effectively; and she promoted within the organization first to recognize the talent and potential that she saw on her team.

She also made every single interaction about the other person because they mattered to her. She saw the bigger picture for each of her team members. To her, they weren't just numbers on reports; they had stories to tell that were truly valuable to her and the company.

See, Mia understood that good leaders engage and build relationships by approaching and engaging with people first. And that you never learn anything about people or their jobs if you do all the talking. She also knew that reports don't always tell the whole story about employees' real-life experiences, their jobs, and the service they give to their customers.

"Good leaders build relationships with others because data reports alone don't show an accurate picture of your business operations."

~Bella Cruz

Mia knew everybody's name. At the beginning of her conversations, she would ask the other person something personal about his or her life; she asked open-ended questions, listened, and took notes while the other person spoke. And after each conversation, Mia always left with something to do. She took employee feedback and made process improvements wherever she could.

She usually spent no more than 10 or 15 minutes with each employee, but in response to Mia's powerful approachability, her employees were always ready to help her — and the organization — with whatever they needed. When Mia met with her employees, it didn't take long because she did this consistently once or twice a week, and she took turns with a few employees at a time.

It takes courage and commitment to the organization for employees to offer feedback. When your team knows that you will honor their input, they will give it to you… and that input is like a gold mine and your key to a thriving workplace.

"Being approachable opens the door for leaders to navigate their careers more successfully, as it shows their managers and colleagues that they matter. When leaders are approachable, they help create a culture of openness and innovation, because team members feel empowered to step outside of their comfort zones with safety."[10]

Principle 3
Be Approachable

The Dos

1) **DO** be approachable

It's not enough for a leader to have a wall of accolades, awards, and degrees. Those are important, but credentials alone cannot motivate your team. If your team feels comfortable approaching you, then you can turn your knowledge, abilities, and experience into teamwork.

"Being approachable is key to building relationships with your colleagues, and to creating a strong team in which trust, confidence, and ideas can flow. When you're approachable, team members do not sit on or cover up problems."[11]

Your employees are a wealth of valuable information about your company's day-to-day operations. Therefore, reports and employee communication will give you a much more accurate assessment of your company than reports alone. But employees can only offer this insight when they feel safe talking to you about it, and when they are confident that you will act and not react to what they tell you.

> "Being approachable is a key that turns a leader's knowledge, abilities, and experience into teamwork."
>
> ~Bella Cruz

2) **DO** have approachable facial expressions

Leadership doesn't just involve focusing on meeting the strategic goals of the company. Connecting with your team is a huge part of leadership influence, and in order to connect with others, you should do what you can to make sure that your team feels comfortable approaching you.

People decide in mere seconds whether or not they are going to approach you. How? By looking at you! Your facial expressions are powerful indicators to others, and your expressions either invite people in or tell them to stay away. Using your facial expressions intentionally is an important life skill. Smiling and maintaining warm, welcoming expressions will skyrocket your success with others. On the other hand, harsh facial expressions will alienate people and limit your ability to communicate and connect with them.

> "Research shows that most people decide whether or not they like someone within the first seven seconds of meeting him or her."[12]

3) DO be sincere

One supervisor I coached said all the right things when he talked to his teams, but he wasn't sincere, and they could tell. They didn't believe him, they didn't like him, and they didn't trust him, which caused a major and costly disconnect.

Showing empathy and caring about people are important leadership characteristics that earn respect. Consistent sincerity is fundamental to being approachable. Sincerity helps you to emotionally connect with people, their ideas, and their contributions so that you can build relationships with them. Humility is a complement to your leadership style. When your employees know that you are sincere, they respond with sincerity. They are inspired and motivated to share insights with you that you need in order to make powerful, effective workplace decisions.

4) **DO** ask for feedback

When employees are not sharing feedback with you, leading is much more difficult. It's like you're wearing glasses with the wrong prescription. You don't have a clear vision of what you need to make the necessary decisions; you don't know what's really going on in the workplace because everything is blurry; and employees are frustrated. They are missing important support resources that you don't know they need; and because they are trying to find their own way through projects, they work at a much slower pace.

On the other hand, asking employees for their feedback is like wearing glasses with the correct prescription. Everything comes into focus, and your vision is clear. You have the information you need so that you and your team can work together with strategic direction.

One of the best ways to get actionable feedback from your team is by asking specific, open-ended questions, which I call *Team Performance Questions*. If you ask a team member, "How are things going?" he or she will probably tell you that "things are fine" or "okay," which doesn't tell you anything that you can act upon. But if you ask someone, "What went well with your job this week?" you will get a different answer with more details. Specific, open-ended questions require the team member to answer you with more than a "yes" or "no." To obtain even more details about a topic, ask: "Tell me more about that…" Open-ended questions elicit those important insights and give you details that help you to make better decisions and better serve your team. These questions also improve engagement and morale because your employees feel like they contributed something.

Here are more *Team Performance Questions* that can help you start a focused conversation about someone's job:

More *Team Performance Questions*

1) What are the customers saying about us?
2) What are some of your recommendations?

"One of the most powerful skills a leader can use to get details about team projects is asking open-ended questions."

~Bella Cruz

5) DO limit technology to emergencies when speaking to others

Technology is part of our everyday lives, personally and professionally. We feel such an urgency to answer when the phone rings or a text message lights up on our phones. This can be a major distraction when we are speaking to others.

Checking your phone, scrolling through emails, or glancing at your watch when someone is speaking to you are definite signs that you're not engaged or listening. Answering a phone call is not just a sign of disinterest, it's nearly a declaration that says, "You're not that important." Most people don't even say "excuse me" anymore when their phone rings; they just dive right into the phone call while someone is sitting right in front of them, trying to talk to them.

I've seen and experienced supervisors who keep working on their computers and even turning their backs to employees during one-on-one meetings. How does that make the other person feel? What does that communicate? In workshops, most employees tell me that they feel like they don't matter. This feeling destroys the motivation to work or collaborate with their supervisor.

However, supervisors do not want their employees to feel like they don't matter. I know that because I've worked, coached, and conducted thousands of leadership workshops. There is a gap between communication and how a supervisor makes an employee feel. The following information will make you aware of the behaviors that can cause some of the communication gaps when having one-on-one meetings with your team. These are comments I've heard over and over again from employees in my workshops.

Answering the questions below can help you to access how you conduct your one-on-one meetings with your team.

ONE-ON-ONE MEETING
Questionnaire for Supervisors

Supervisors: Describe in the blank boxes what body language, gestures, and communication styles you would use to change the following scenarios into positive and productive meetings with employees.

1	"I don't know why my supervisor even bothers meeting with me! They don't even give me the time of day."	
2	"When I meet with my supervisor, they answer phone calls or scroll through their phone during our meetings. I feel invisible!"	
3	"My supervisor turns their back to me and starts working on their computer during our meetings. That is so rude! Why do they even meet with me?"	
4	"Meeting with my boss is so frustrating. They don't care about me or my job. They do all the talking and just tell me what to do."	
5	"My boss is so rude. They cancel our meetings all the time. When we finally meet, they say they only have a few minutes because they have to leave for another meeting."	
6	"My supervisor ignores my emails and phone calls, and they hardly ever communicate with me. I don't feel like I'm part of the team, and I feel uncomfortable when I meet with them."	

Book Source: *Please Fire Me! I Can't Stand My Boss (How Today's Leaders Build Relationships, Job Satisfaction & Retention)* by Bella Cruz © 2021. Leadership Coaching & Workshops: www.Created2lead.com

The comments above in the *One-on-one Meeting Questionnaire for Supervisors* are real. How you treat people when you are talking to them makes all the difference in the world. They will either be engaged or disengaged with you, depending on how you treat them.

Remember that your most important asset is your employees. They were hired by you to help you and the company succeed. The human connection is a fundamental piece of engagement. Recognize this, and your team's morale will skyrocket through the roof.

6) DO learn about your employees

When I visit my doctor, she always makes me feel special by asking me something about my personal life. This is one of the best ways to build relationships, and it doesn't take long for us to connect!

One day, I mentioned to her how impressed I was that she remembers details about me. She told me her secret: she makes notes in her patients' charts to help her connect and build relationships with them faster. This helps her to better care for her patients because, when she connects with them, they are more open with her about their health.

She suggested that I write notes in my phone under my clients' contact information; that way, when I meet with them again, I can better and more quickly connect with them. This simple technique, done with sincerity, is well worth the time. People appreciate it when we remember something about *them*. Getting to know your employees communicates to them that they matter, and when they know that they matter to you, you become more approachable to them. They will feel more comfortable coming to you to ask questions, and they will naturally become more engaged.

People are usually already telling you about their personal life. All you have to do is look at people's desks, pictures, or office walls to get an idea of what they like or what is interesting to them. Then ask them about it!

7) **DO be aware of your communication style**

Many supervisors are not aware of their communication style… but they should be. Let's face it. Who is going to tell their supervisor if they can't communicate effectively with them. Some employees will do anything to avoid talking to their supervisor because they make the employee feel incompetent, they offend them, they talk down to them, or they say things to them that make them angry or upset.

If your tone of voice and body language change depending on who you are talking to at the moment, then you have conscious control of those things, which means that you can choose to convey positive messages.

Becoming self-aware and being intentional about improving your communication style can change your world. To help you improve your leadership skills, you can take leadership training, hire a coach or mentor, or take any one of the 360 leadership or personality assessments available. Personality and communication assessments can help you identify your strengths and blind spots so that you can become more approachable and connect better with your team(s).

> "Leadership is the ability to get extraordinary achievements from ordinary people."
>
> ~ Brian Tracy

Leadership Questions

1) How do you show your employees that they matter?

_____

_____

_____

2) What questions do you ask your team members to obtain details about their jobs and what your customers are saying about your services?

_____

_____

_____

Principle 3
Be Approachable

The "What's in It for Me?" Leader

Earlier in this book, I named two areas in which I saw the greatest lack — and the greatest importance — in the corporate world. They are **trust** and **accountability**. Time and again, these two qualities have proven the most effective makers or breakers of any company, large or small.

Imagine yourself as an employee in your organization who has important questions about your most recent project before it can move forward. But every time you see your supervisor, his or her entire energy tells you, "I don't have time for you." Would you trust him or her to answer your questions thoroughly and respectfully?

Louis Wright was an ambitious supervisor with his sights set on a senior executive position, which was more or less his all-consuming obsession. He exuded the "World revolves around me!" energy. He once said to me, "I don't do anything unless there's something in it for me!" And he meant it!

That "anything" he "didn't do" included communicating with his employees with a cold, quick "Hi, how are you?" without any eye contact when passing them quickly in the hallway. He spoke in short, impatient sentences, usually demanding, and sounding, like this: "Where are you on this project?" "Do such-and-such." "Just take care of it." "I need that from you today." "Where is so-and-so?" or "Where is everybody when I need them?" His sharp tone of voice and distant body language were warning signs to employees that sent them scattering. His department had a rampant turnover rate, and even his fellow supervisors only worked with him when they needed him to be involved.

Louis wasn't just distant when communicating; he was uninvolved and absent. His manager, who was really the one in charge, conducted most of his meetings on his behalf. If Louis did show up to a meeting, he was late, he dominated the discussion, and he misunderstood the *silence of his team* as engagement with what he was saying. At the end of the meeting, he would ask if anyone had questions, wait for a beat, and then declare that the meeting was over and rush out of the room. He didn't know that silence is not golden in the workplace.

Something is wrong within the team when employees are silent and not asking questions. They might not be comfortable approaching you for one reason or another; maybe they're intimidated, or they fear you, or maybe they don't feel supported, or maybe they've completely checked out, or maybe they're looking for another job and don't care anymore. No matter the reason, let me repeat: their silence is not golden. Open lines of communication are essential to daily workplace operations, and in order for them to stay open, you must make yourself approachable to your employees.

"Leadership is knowing that silence is not golden when it comes to team dynamics."

~ Bella Cruz

Principle 3
Be Approachable

The Don'ts

1) DON'T have a "what's in it for me?" attitude

When someone has the "I don't do anything unless it benefits me" attitude, he or she is focused on getting ahead at whatever cost. These people work alone. If they are a supervisor, the team works alone too, because it has no support, which leads to a disengaged and mentally absent team. This type of leader misses the opportunities to tap into the team's talents, solutions, and ideas. The leader is not growing, and neither is his or her influence.

"… A Gallup poll of more than one million employed U.S. workers concluded that the number one reason people quit their jobs is a bad boss or immediate supervisor. Some 75% of workers who voluntarily left their jobs did so because of their bosses and not the position itself."[13]

It is important to be involved in helping others and empowering individuals to become leaders themselves. Your world opens up when you stop working alone and start working united. This is called synergy!

2) DON'T blame others

Unfortunately, many supervisors make comments like the following to their leaders, peers, and their employees in order to blame others: "Who did this?"; "This is the first time I hear about this!"; "I didn't approve that!"; "The department is understaffed"; "They are supposed to be working on that…" or they use the word "they" instead of "we."

This is a "blame them" supervisor. High-trust, accountable leaders will always look for ways to help and support their team. They are compassionate and courageous, and they are always looking for what they can do instead of focusing on what others haven't done.

Be proactive! Use positive language to motivate your employees so that they can help you create a healthy, high-trust culture of accountability in the workplace.

3) DON'T be an absent leader

An employee once told me that someone on the team would go to the movies and shop during work hours because the supervisor was never around. Other employees told me that they didn't talk to their boss for months at a time, or that they'd only talk to them during performance evaluations because their boss was absent, unapproachable or didn't feel that they knew their job. This leadership style keeps morale low and discourages employees from leaning into their positions.

"Our research also revealed that 53% of
employees who don't trust their managers feel
this way because their managers 'don't appear to
know what they are doing.'"[14]

Create a strong relationship with your team so
that they can approach you when they need your support.
Open lines of communication turn rework costs and
mistakes into job satisfaction and autonomy.

Leadership Questions

1) How do you engage your teams to communicate with you?

   _____

   _____

   _____

2) How do employees react to you when you walk into the room? Do they approach you, or do they walk the other way? For what reason?

   _____

   _____

   _____

Principle 4
Don't Have Favorites

Hire the Right People!

William Washington understood the importance of healthy team dynamics. He knew that it started internally; after all, leaders lead by example. He continuously embraced opportunities to develop himself professionally and worked often with mentors so that he could coach his employees into an award-winning team.

Along with self-development, William knew that hiring the right people was also crucial to healthy team dynamics. He kept job descriptions current and met with other managers to optimize the interview process. It was a time investment, but it helped to find the right person for the job, which minimized turnover and unnecessary training.

> "According to a benchmark report from SHRM, the average cost per hire across organizations and industries is $4,125 dollars. But to calculate the cost of onboarding a new employee, you must also factor in the costs mentioned…
>
> • The hours managers spend training new employees—average cost: $1,296 per employee
> • Paper, printing, and office supplies—average annual cost: between $922 and $1,106
> • Training—$1,252 per employee on average"[15]

William also kept the dynamics of his team members healthy by prioritizing their self-development as well as his own. He secured a training and development budget for each of his employees, and he held all employees accountable for their development by requiring them to set professional goals for themselves that would make use of their new skills. William also brainstormed new goals with them, ensuring that they were always moving toward the fullest expression of their potential.

William also worked with the entire team to focus on building relationships with them. The more he worked with them, the more confidence they gained in their abilities. This caused the team members to discover how to contribute and find powerful performance solutions for their jobs.

> "… employees who thought their leaders were more empowering were indeed more likely to feel empowered at work — they felt a greater sense of autonomy or control in their work, they felt that their job had meaning, and it aligned with their values, that they were competent in their abilities, and that they could make a difference…"[16]

Did all of his employees engage in the development process? No. There will always be employees who don't want to change their current state in life. Self-development is an investment, and like any investment, it is a risk; but it's a risk well worth taking. Those who do engage reap rewards for themselves, their peers, their leadership, their organizations, and their team.

Principle 4
Don't Have Favorites

The Dos

1) **DO be aware of the "favorites" syndrome**

Favoritism is more common than most leaders want to admit. In the thousands of workshops, face-to-face interviews, and surveys I conducted in my 25-year career, favoritism was the number one complaint that employees voiced about their supervisors. And because it is so pervasive — and destructive — it is *extremely* important not to demonstrate favoritism in the workplace.

Supervisors can help eliminate favoritism by becoming more aware of their behavior toward employees. Giving certain employees better treatment will create resentment, undermine loyalty, and divide the team.

> "The consequences of favoritism were numerous. Employees not only deemed favoritism as a form of workplace injustice/unfairness, but also reacted to favoritism behaviors with negative emotions toward the organization, less loyalty to the company, less job satisfaction, stronger intentions to quit the job, less work motivation, and more emotional exhaustion."[17]

2) **DO have a standardized, effective hiring process**

Many supervisors rush to fill positions without checking to see if they have current job descriptions that will help identify the best candidate. Some supervisors also trust their first impressions and fail to ask the right questions, and others don't have any kind of standardized hiring process. The following tips can help you set up a process to find the right person for each position.

a. DO have accurate and updated job descriptions

One of my worst workplace experiences happened when I was an employee, before I started my own business. I accepted a job that was nothing like the job description. I left after a few months because I was so miserable. Think of the resources that the firm spent training me; think of the wasted time, mine and theirs alike. I can personally attest to the feelings of frustration and mistrust I experienced as an employee. Creating the right job description can help you hire the right person and save you (and others) money, time, and frustration.

Take the time to review job descriptions with your management team. Ask your team questions about the workplace positions to keep your job descriptions current. Determine if you need to add new responsibilities, technologies, adjusted pay, etc.

b. **DO use behavioral interview questions**

Behavioral, open-ended interview questions require candidates to give you specific examples about their work history and describe their unique experiences, such as how they've solved problems, promoted teamwork, or earned awards. Be strategic and create questions that help you understand whether the candidate has a track record of skills that are important for the position you're filling. Asking all interviewees the same questions helps you to compare their answers more accurately in order to identify who among them is the best fit for your company. Work with your human resources department to make sure that you follow all company interview policies.

> "…[behavioral interview] questions can provide the interviewer with insight into your personality, skills, and abilities. Because each behavioral interview question requires you to share a specific story that highlights your strengths and skills, thoughtful preparation can help you feel confident and prepared."[18]

c. **DO** ask potential hires if they have any questions

Pay close attention when you ask interviewees if they have any questions. Were they proactive in researching the company ahead of time? Are they asking questions about the team, the culture, or your expectations for the job? Did they ask about self-development or training opportunities? Inquisitive candidates usually stand out from the rest of the candidates.

No hiring process guarantees that you will always hire the right employees. Some people don't work out or they decide to leave. However, planning and spending time creating the right questions for your interviews can help you find the candidate with the right skills for the job.

> "People are not your most important asset. The right people are."
>
> ~ Jim Collins

3) **DO** create a professional development plan for employees

If you're not learning anything new, actively trying to get better at your job, reading books, attending conferences or webinars, or working with a mentor or coach… then chances are good that your team isn't, either. Training is indispensable in a high-trust culture of accountability. A supervisor who is not taking the initiative to improve his or her own professional skills, and doesn't see the importance of self-development training, rarely provides these opportunities to the team.

If you don't have the budget for training at this time, there are many free training resources like YouTube videos, online webinars, and online libraries. You can also promote cross-training and encourage employees to join committees to gain experience and learn new skills. Helping others discover a new level of their potential makes employees feel like you recognize their ability to contribute. It also creates a balance within the team, instead of relying on a few certain people to get the job done.

4) **DO discover the potential on your team**

"Knowing the strengths and weaknesses of every individual to effectively manage the outcome of a team is imperative for success. Leaders have a great vision and use the resources at hand to solve problems."[19]

An effective leader learns the team's strengths and blind spots and provides coaching, mentoring, and training. This helps accelerate team performance to greater levels of productivity and job satisfaction.

5) **DO treat all employees with the same respect**

Motivating and engaging your team requires respecting people. And that doesn't just involve being polite to them. True respect, the kind that makes itself known, means taking the time to find out what motivates and inspires people by asking them about their dreams, fears, and struggles in the workplace. Knowing and acting on this information helps both you and your employees better understand how to grow toward success.

Your respectful conduct toward your employees is important to them. Most employees want to make a difference and do well in their jobs, but they also want you to care about them and to show them that their job matters. It's a simple concept, but unfortunately not always common. Be humble enough to acknowledge that you need the team to help you do your job to meet the company's goals. When your employees know that their contribution matters, and that you see that it matters, you will motivate them more than any seminar or conference ever could.

> "In a study of nearly 20,000 employees around the world (conducted with [Harvard Business Review] HBR),… Being treated with respect was more important to employees than recognition and appreciation, communicating an inspiring vision, providing useful feedback — or even opportunities for learning, growth, and development."[20]

6) **DO** maintain the same boundaries for everyone

Since childhood, most of us have seen or been the favorite at home with our families, at school with teachers and coaches, or in the workplace with supervisors. Everyone knows who the "favorites" are without anyone having to say a word. Have the same boundaries and rules for everyone on your team to avoid the perception of having favorites.

Leadership Questions

1) What characteristics do you demonstrate in your leadership style to prevent having favorites in the workplace?

_____

_____

_____

2) What criteria do you use to provide the right professional development opportunities to all your team members?

_____

_____

_____

Principle 4
Don't Have Favorites

The "I Have My Favorites" Leader

As early as my first meeting with Tom Reynolds, I could see why I'd been brought in to coach him. Nothing about him personally was wrong, but just passing his team between the front door and his office was awkward. They were so cold to him that it felt like the temperature had dropped fifteen degrees. In a matter of seconds, I could diagnose the major disconnect.

Tom and I walked to another part of the building to start our coaching sessions. It didn't take long for Tom to acknowledge the tension he was experiencing. Only minutes into our meeting, Tom was in tears as he described to me the legal action brought against him by his team that had recently been keeping him up at night.

The culprit? Favoritism.

Tom was an executive director with a team of 50 people, but to him, 49 of them stopped existing once Gina Morgan entered the room. It would have been difficult not to notice her, though. She was a top performer and a creative problem solver. She met deadlines consistently, came in early, stayed late, and proactively sought out learning opportunities. When it came down to results, her projects performed the best! It was no mystery why she stood out to Tom.

Soon, Gina became his right-hand person. Wherever he was, so was she: walking down the hall, driving to other company campuses, and even going on business trips with him. Gina also started getting high-profile projects because she began attending client meetings with him; despite lacking the experience of her peers. She got the office with the window, without the job description that came with it, and she had exclusive access to Tom. She had a lot of favor with Tom, and everyone noticed.

> "In a survey study with 303 U.S. executives[1], they found that more than half (56 percent) of executives admitted to having a favorite candidate when making internal promotion decisions, and 96 percent of them will promote their favorites rather than considering the candidates' communication abilities, which is crucial for the position examined in the study."[21]

Tom also became a different person when Gina was around. His voice changed when he spoke to her. Instead of harsh indistinct orders, he spoke politely, and he showered her with praise. Everyone noticed.

Tom was even more receptive to Gina's ideas. Tom once dismissed a suggestion from one employee, only to reconsider it when Gina made the recommendation sometime later. And, of course, again everyone noticed.

Tom's team finally began to retaliate. Some only let their frustration out as passive aggression. They acted kindly, but sabotaged Gina's work behind the scenes by canceling meetings with her, keeping important information from her, and isolating her from the rest of the team. Others expressed their resentment right in front of her with remarks like, "Gina's the superstar — let her figure it out by herself!" Not only did they do just that, but they also served Tom with a serious favoritism lawsuit.

How much work do you think this office produced since Tom's favoritism started? Resentment had simmered long enough that it came to a full-blown boil, and now it was spilling over in every direction. Not even the most efficient worker could produce anything in such a toxic culture. Favoritism doesn't just cost the organization revenue; it quickly translates into turnover, too.

"If you think you are leading and turn around and see no one is following, then you are just taking a walk."

~Benjamin Hooks

Empower your entire team and motivate them to work together in a way that utilizes each of their strengths. When you recognize everyone's abilities, they will also recognize each other's strengths and collaborate effectively.

Principle 4
Don't Have Favorites

The Don'ts

1) **DON'T have favorites**

When a supervisor has a favorite employee, it is painfully obvious. During meetings or team gatherings, the supervisor's attention is always directed at the favorite instead of the entire team. Some supervisors even create new positions to promote their favorite employees or give them better offices and privileges.

"Employees not only deemed favoritism as a form of workplace injustice/unfairness, but also reacted to favoritism behaviors with negative emotions toward the organization, less loyalty to the company, less job satisfaction, stronger intentions to quit the job, less work motivation, and more emotional exhaustion."[22]

Everyone on your team is watching, so the negative energy begins to seep into the team when there is a favorite(s). It's like being in a stadium full of people and you're the main event on stage. All eyes are on you!

There are consequences... The company's mission and vision priorities take a back seat because the focus shifts to the relationship between the leader and the favorite or favorites. Some obvious favoritism behaviors include:

a. Visiting the favorite at his or her work area

It's so awkward when supervisors rush past other employees to visit their favorite in the workplace. Everyone knows where they're going because they do it all the time. Now, the supervisor and the favorite are the main focus of the workplace instead of the company priorities.

Build a collaborative and unified team. Distribute work according to roles and responsibilities, and encourage and reward teamwork. When your team members feel like they're all working together, instead of competing with one another, they will excel.

b. Behind-the-scenes behavior toward the favorite

Most supervisors don't realize that favoritism actually has negative consequences for the "favorite employee" too. Employees may be nice to the favorite employee in person or in front of the supervisor, but when the supervisor's back is turned, the relationship between the favorite and the team is dysfunctional.

Most employees isolate the favorite employee. Just like Gina's team, they cancel project meetings, they delay responding to emails and phone calls, or they avoid interacting with the favorite altogether. Some employees even sabotage the favorite's work. The favorite employee can start feeling the pressure of having to work on high-profile projects with little or no support from the team. This type of team dynamics can also cause the favorite employee to leave the company.

Create a culture of cohesiveness and engage the employees by rewarding teamwork. Respect all employees, treat them the same based on their roles and responsibilities, and give them an opportunity to excel at their jobs.

2) DON'T give special access to certain employees

During one team meeting I attended, the team's supervisor was running late. The employees began asking if anyone had heard from her. The employee who everyone called the "golden child" pulled out his phone to call the supervisor because she had given him her private cell phone number. It got everyone's attention. When everyone looked his way, he just smiled.

An individual's ego can create negative energy and conflict for the entire team, especially when the supervisor's special treatment has given him or her a sense of entitlement.

Create a positive, high-trust culture of accountability by strengthening your entire team. Unite them, communicate with them, and collaborate with them.

3) DON'T hang out with employees

Have you seen supervisors hanging out with their favorite employees in the cafeteria, sitting with them at lunch, texting them, traveling with them to meetings or on business trips, or going to happy hour with them? This behavior does not go unnoticed by the other team members. Employees feel excluded, which is devastating to morale.

4) DON'T share leadership information

Favoritism also manifests in sharing confidential leadership information with someone who does not have the authority to know it. This includes upcoming budget decisions, pending policies or projects, or personal information about yourself or other team members. Gossiping is also deadly to morale, and it can cause employees to disrespect you as their leader.

How do you know if you're doing this? The favorite employee hears comments like: "Between you and me," "Now, don't say anything to anyone else," or "This is confidential."

Be a positive, high-trust, accountable leader and create a communication process to share information with the entire team at the same time.

5) DON'T leave anyone out

I have heard so many employees express frustration about being left out... not included in emails, excluded from meetings, or not invited to office luncheons or celebrations. Many employees also complain about being forgotten by supervisors when they are handing out awards or incentives to the team. Ouch! I could always hear the hurt or anger in employees' voices when they talked about it. Supervisors don't usually exclude them on purpose, but it can still cause employees to resent them when it does happen.

The great news is that being intentional can prevent these scenarios. Scheduling events on your calendar, and making distribution lists and checklists, are some things that can help ensure that everyone is included.

6) FOLLOW your Human Resources department policies

Employees sometimes file HR grievances against supervisors when they experience favoritism in the workplace. The process is time-consuming, stressful, and very costly for the company.

> "Favoritism creates a wedge in the team. It breaks the sense of unity that most teams have. When one person is a favorite, the others will not take it lightly, and then the gossiping and unhealthy competition follows. There is no real winner in this scenario because when the team loses, the organization loses..."[23]

Take the time to discover what each employee contributes to the team and how everyone can work together to create an environment of positive accountability. Develop the team so that it utilizes each member's talents.

Disclaimer: In my 25-year coaching and speaking career, I have seen employees file grievances against their supervisors for favoritism. But I am not a lawyer, and I am not giving legal advice. I am only making you aware of the potential consequences of favoritism. Speak to your HR department to learn your company's specific policies.

Leadership Questions

1) How do you partner with your human resources office to stay current with policies and avoid issues with employees?

_____

_____

_____

2) How do you avoid leaving an employee out of team activities, emails, or awards, etc.?

_____

_____

_____

Principle 5
Tell Me What Accountability
Looks Like

Accountability in the Workplace!

A ccountable leaders attract top performers and retain their employees. They create united teams because they can communicate clearly with their employees to motivate, engage, and ensure greater levels of productivity and profits. How? They are intentional about modeling and documenting what positive accountability performance behaviors look like in the workplace. Effective leaders build these behaviors into their processes, and they create an *Accountability Performance Model* © that helps guide their employees in fulfilling their duties. An accountable leader also demonstrates accountability behaviors consistently.

Yet, one of the greatest challenges leaders face today is accountability in the workplace. Why? Because supervisors find it difficult to bring up the issue with their teams. They see it as conflict, or they only bring it up when someone does something wrong. What happens when someone says to you, "We need to talk about accountability?" For most people, it feels like their stomach just dropped to the floor. Their thoughts start racing: "What did I do wrong?" "Am I going to get fired?"

This is why the word "accountability" has a negative connotation with most leaders and employees. Some supervisors avoid holding their employees accountable altogether, which results in keeping an employee who is not a good fit for the company. Other supervisors get so busy with their deadlines, responsibilities, and priorities that they don't see the issues within their team until the problems escalate. When this happens, nothing changes, and the problems persist. The results affect individual employee performance, team dynamics, productivity, and the company's ROI (return on investment).

> "Holding people accountable is difficult—even for leaders who head up companies. Eighteen percent of the CEOs we surveyed cited "holding people accountable" as their biggest weakness. Additionally, 15 percent struggle with "letting go of underperformers."[24]

Clear communication of work expectations is the first step on the journey of employee accountability. Outlining goals and metrics for successful outcomes provides your team with a roadmap for how its success will look, and meeting with them often to communicate and collaborate keeps them engaged.

Principle 5
Tell Me What Accountability
Looks Like

The "Accountable" Leader

That first dose of accountability after a lack of it for so long is a breath of fresh air. And I don't mean a deep breath in a light spring breeze... I mean a deep gulp of air when you've been underwater for five minutes! An injection of accountability revitalizes your organization.

Matthew Del Ray experienced this firsthand. When I started working with Matthew, he was a well-established executive at one of the most successful companies in the world. His leadership team consisted of other executives, directors, and managers who supervised more than 25,000 employees.

But this company was not always built on such a solid foundation. When Matthew first arrived, he scheduled a meeting where department leaders were asked to make presentations about their roles and responsibilities that included metrics and budgets. The department leaders and hundreds of team members would meet in an enormous auditorium to see the first glimpse of Matthew's leadership style.

From the moment the meeting began, the energy of the organization shifted. Matthew listened to each presentation intently and offered each presenter his undivided attention. After the first presenter finished discussing his metrics, he politely asked him to pause, and everyone held their breath. The room was so silent that even those in the very back row could hear the sound of Matthew's typing.

Then he said, "Your metrics are current and correct. Please continue."

"In one study they found that 84% of employees surveyed said the way leaders behave is the single most important factor influencing accountability in their organizations."[25]

With these few words, Matthew ushered in a new era of *accountability* for this company. Everyone let out a sigh and looked at each other in amazement, but they were a changed group. Managers and supervisors soon began scheduling regular accountability meetings to ensure that all the reports, the company's information, and even the website was kept up to date. Posters were also taken down and replaced with updated and more professional ones. Everyone was in compliance mode, almost as if they were expecting an audit. And no one even had to be told; everyone just knew that they were now an accountable organization. Matthew held himself and others accountable, and accountability performance became the priority for excellence.

But this atmosphere shift didn't come with the stiff legalism that often accompanies compliance. Matthew prioritized accountability, but he partnered it with *trust*. He made it a priority to connect not only with his leadership teams, but with employees at all levels as well. Sometimes he would walk into the cafeteria and go into the kitchen to greet the employees, or he would stop and talk to those waiting by the time clock before their shifts.

As a part of the company's new accountability initiative, Matthew asked his leadership team to create a tool called the *Accountability Performance Model* ©. This model puts into writing the accountability behaviors that you expect from your teams to help employees do their jobs. This simple, but revolutionary tool helps guide teams by describing what positive and negative accountability behaviors look like in the workplace. Matthew understood the importance of providing his employees with an illustration of specific accountability behaviors. This model was posted in breakrooms and on the company Intranet so that everyone could easily access it. Matthew's *Accountability Performance Model* © and leadership style helped transform workplace conduct.

Matthew created a culture of accountability and trust; he empowered and cared about his teams, and they cared about him. He was a transformational, influential leader who left a legacy.

> "Leadership is unlocking people's potential to become better."
>
> ~ Bill Bradle

Principle 5
Tell Me What Accountability Looks Like

The Dos

1) **DO** take the initiative to improve your leadership skills

If you don't lead your team, an "unofficial leader" will fill that role. But that unofficial leader doesn't always know what he or she is doing.

You are the best person to lead your team, but you can always lead them *better.* When you invest in self-development training, you also encourage your team to do the same. When you inspire others to reach their highest potential, you improve processes for the team and the customers.

"If you are indecisive and do not step up to take action, someone on your team will eventually do it for you. The result over time will be that team members will stop coming to you for decisions because you take too long and instead, they will ask the "unofficial leader" of your team what to do."[26]

2) DO create an *Accountability Performance Model* ©

I've heard many supervisors complain about employee accountability, but those same supervisors have not shown their employees what accountability looks like in the workplace! Your employees will know that accountability is a priority in your company — and they will know how to demonstrate it — when you provide them with an *Accountability Performance Model* ©. Displaying this model helps employees to model positive workplace accountability behaviors.

How do I know that most supervisors don't have an *Accountability Performance Model* © for their employees? I've asked them! In hundreds of workshops, I've asked participants, "How many of you have an accountability model for your employees?" In a room filled with dozens of people, maybe two raise their hands. The most common reasons supervisors give me for not having an *Accountability Performance Model* © in the workplace are:

1) Supervisors have never seen one.
2) Supervisors are too busy to create one.

I've created an *Accountability Performance Model* © that outlines the fundamental dos and don'ts of accountability. This model is the product of the thousands of workshops I've conducted with hundreds of thousands of supervisors and employees in my 25 years of experience as a leadership coach and strategist.

You can use the *Accountability Performance Model* © below with your teams. Add your logo, modify it to fit your company culture, or use it as a guide to create your own model.

If you need help creating an *Accountability Performance Model* © please contact our team at www.created2lead.com.

ACCOUNTABILITY
Performance Model©

Dos	DON'Ts
BE ACCOUNTABLE • Use positive integrity and character • Respect others, company values, policies, and procedures • Take ownership of your work • Ask for help when needed	**BE A VICTIM** • Make excuses • Ignore or blame others • Avoid asking for help • Avoid responsibility
KEEP PROMISES • Make promises within your control • Follow through with your promises • Communicate when keeping promises is not possible	**BREAK PROMISES** • Make promises you know you won't keep • Make promises out of your control
COMMUNICATE OPENLY • Ask for and give feedback • Demonstrate positive communication • Keep others informed • Listen to understand the other person • Have a positive attitude	**COMMUNICATE NEGATIVELY** • Be afraid to ask questions • Ignore communicating with others • Have a negative attitude
DEMONSTATE TEAMWORK • Inspire and encourage others • Help others • Work as a team • Celebrate and be happy for others	**CREATE DIVISION** • Isolate yourself from the team • Ignore celebrating others • Gossip or talk negatively about others
CONTRIBUTE TO PROBLEM SOLVING • Share ideas to create synergy • Provide solutions • Make recommendations • Encourage others	**BLOCK PROBLEM SOLVING** • Stay silent during team activities • Complain about the process • Keep your potential to yourself
REINVENT FAILURES INTO SUCCESSES • See failures as new opportunities • Use failures as lessons learned • Have the courage to change direction	**BE AFRAID OF FAILURE** • Let fear win • Give up • Discourage others • Look at challenges as failures

Book Source: *Please Fire Me! I Can't Stand My Boss (How Today's Leaders Build Relationships, Job Satisfaction & Retention)* by Bella Cruz © 2021. Leadership coaching & workshops: www.created2lead.com

3) **DO** provide accountability performance training

When presented positively, accountability training frequently becomes one of the most popular training programs in any company. High-trust accountability training has always been one of my most requested workshops by supervisors and employees. At conferences, I have even been added to more than one session because it is such a popular topic.

It is important to have on-demand online or instructor-led accountability training in the workplace. Even providing training in small increments in staff meetings or huddles with supervisors can make a giant impact on your team performance and employee engagement if done consistently.

Here's how:

1) During your staff meetings, schedule a five- or ten-minute agenda item for self-development.

2) Take one of the behaviors from your *Accountability Performance Model* © and briefly talk about it with your team at each of your staff meetings. Consider focusing on an accountability behavior relevant to a project that week.

3) Ask your employees to give examples of how they would use that accountability behavior positively in the workplace or when working on a project with the team. If employees bring up a negative issue, ask them what they learned and how they would turn it into a positive example.

These simple training ideas help the team stay engaged; they learn what positive accountability behaviors look like and how to implement them in the workplace. Because the team is receiving training that helps them self-discover what they are learning, they can begin practicing it immediately. This causes them to be engaged at a deeper level, and the learning is more solidly cemented.

"Leadership is transforming unproductive meetings into ideas, collaboration, personal and team accountability, and productivity."

~ Bella Cruz

4) DO document accountability performance behaviors for sustainment

It's important to start communicating your *Accountability Performance Model* © as soon as employees are hired to help guide them on what positive accountability behaviors look like within your company. The accountability performance behaviors can be outlined in the following materials:

1) New hire (employee) orientation
2) Employee handbook
3) Standard operating procedures (SOPs) or policies
4) Performance evaluation criteria
5) Display your *Accountability Performance Model* © in your break rooms, offices, or at employees' desks

Note: It is extremely important that your executive leaders and human resources (HR) office approve your company's accountability performance training and models before presenting them to your employees. The topic of accountability should *always* be communicated safely and positively, and it should align with your company's policies and guidelines. Creating your own *Accountability Performance Model* © using your company's policies and values can help your teams understand what accountability behaviors look like in the workplace.

5) Avoid HR grievances by following HR rules

Putting someone on a performance improvement plan (PIP) takes supervisors away from other work priorities because they have to spend time documenting an employee's performance in writing, making phone calls, writing emails, and providing training to the employee, etc. They also spend a lot of time meeting with HR representatives during the process.

Having accountability performance behaviors in the workplace can help prevent some accountability issues because they are a compass for personal responsibility that can increase job satisfaction and morale.

Take the time on the front end to document accountability behaviors and show your team what success looks like to you and the company. This can give you extra hours in your day to concentrate on your strategic priorities instead of having to concentrate on HR issues with employees.

Leadership Questions

1) How do you hold yourself accountable to your team(s)?

_____

_____

_____

2) How does your team know what accountability behaviors looks like in the workplace?

_____

_____

_____

Principle 5
Tell Me What Accountability Looks Like

The "Read My Mind" Leader

Cindy Martin walked out of her supervisor's office with tears flowing down her cheeks. I stopped her to make sure that she was okay and asked her what was wrong. She said, "My boss just wrote me up for something I didn't even know I was doing wrong. If she had just talked to me, I would have changed it."

> "Only 40% of employees report that they are well informed about their company's goals, strategies, and tactics."[27]

The reason Cindy was written up was because she wanted to get lunch for everyone. She knew that she probably wouldn't make it back during her 30-minute lunch break, so she asked a friend to use her badge to clock her back in at the 30-minute mark. Cindy didn't know that doing this was against company policy.

The director of the call center where Cindy worked was Nancy Falls. She did not think that it was her job to tell her employees what was and was not acceptable in the workplace. "They should know already," she would say; "Geez... That's common sense!"; The team should know their jobs!"; "Just take care of it. It's your job!"; or "If I have to show people how to do their job, why don't I just do it myself!" This is the "Read My Mind" leader!

Cindy wasn't the only victim of Nancy's hands-off leadership style. None of her employees were properly trained, so they made a lot of mistakes... mistakes that carried hefty penalties for the company. If they had questions, they knew how Nancy felt about helping them, and the comments she would make, so they asked their coworkers for help instead. If they didn't know how to help the customers, sometimes they would just hang up on them. This made the customers angry because they would have to call back, wait a long time on the phone for someone to answer, and then have to explain all over again what service they needed. You can imagine what a bad impression this left on the call center's customers.

> "A study done in an IDC white paper estimated the average annual cost of "employee misunderstanding" — defined as mistakes caused by employees misunderstanding or misinterpreting operations, job functions, and policies — as $62.4 million."[28]

All of Nancy's time at work was consumed by customer complaints and emails from her boss about her employees' behavior. But when pressed about why she didn't hold her employees accountable, all she had to say was, "They should know already," as if the employees could read her mind! She made excuses and left her team to fend for themselves. Eventually, Nancy was fired for her inability to lead.

Leaders, take nothing for granted. Whether you are a seasoned leader or a first-time supervisor, you can learn what it takes to motivate employees to show up and perform at their best and to embrace personal accountability in the workplace. Your team will flourish in the boundaries you build for them.

> "Accountability leaders hold themselves accountable first."
>
> ~ Bella Cruz

Principle 5
Tell Me What Accountability Looks Like

The Don'ts

1) DON'T ignore accountability performance behaviors in the workplace

When employees know that they are on the radar for poor performance, it's hard for them to concentrate on anything else. They feel like they are on thin ice. Their work starts to suffer even more because of overwhelming thoughts like, "Why am I failing?" "Will I lose my job?" and "How will I provide for my family?" And because the rest of the team takes notice, they begin to fear that they're next, which causes everyone's performance and productivity to falter.

When employees are unhappy and caught up in their own minds instead of focused on their work, your customers will sense the tension. They will be unhappy too. Take the time to create an *Accountability Performance Model* © to help avoid these awkward behaviors. Model success for your employees so that they know what it looks like to be successful at their jobs.

2) DON'T ignore accountability performance training

When there is no accountability performance training available in your organization, it's like the employees are going through a maze trying to figure out what and what is not acceptable to the company and the supervisor. This is wasted, unfocused time. Responsible leaders don't ignore training. They recognize the benefit of employees gaining clarity, improving their skills, and increasing their self-awareness. Training increases production, reduces errors, and helps employees gain the confidence to ask for help.

"Research shows that 40 percent of employees who don't receive necessary training will leave their positions within the first year and 87 percent of millennials cited access to professional development as being a very important factor to their decision to stay or go. … In 2018, $87.6 billion was spent on training expenditures for U.S.-based corporations."[29]

Leadership Questions

1) What accountability training do you provide to your employees?

_____

_____

_____

2) How do you know that your teams know how to perform their jobs accurately?

_____

_____

_____

Principle 6
Communicate Clear
Project Expectations

GPS Leadership

One of the best leaders and communicators I have met during my coaching events was Elizabeth Nguyen. Her communication style was engaging and inviting. She was intentional and, when she spoke, it was as if she had selected every word she said to paint a clear picture for her team to understand what everyone was supposed to do in their jobs.

Elizabeth asked open-ended questions to collect important data from the team and listened to understand to make sure that all questions from her employees were answered. Why? Because you only get answers and information to the questions you ask.

Elizabeth empowered and encouraged her team to create a culture that benefited everyone. She was a great communicator and role model, and the team performed to its highest capacity because communication, trust, and accountability were high. This created buy-in from the team towards Elizabeth's leadership, and buy-in makes the engine of the organization flow in the same direction. Why? Because employees buy-in to the leader first… then to their jobs and the organization.

I like to compare Elizabeth's leadership style to a GPS. You trust the GPS because it has consistently taken you where you asked it to take you, and you've arrived at your destination over and over again. This is similar to consistent, dedicated, and successful leadership. The GPS also shows you a picture of where you are going before you get there. You can see the big picture of what's right in front of you in detail, depending on how you adjust the screen: this is like the supervisor communicating clearly the organization's vision and the roles and responsibilities for each team member.

The GPS communicates with you throughout your entire journey, like supervisors who clearly communicate often with their employees. Even when you are not familiar with your destination, you can depend on that GPS to get you where you are going. This is similar to employees who trust their leaders to help them and show them how to do their jobs. The GPS also gets you to your destination, close to the time it predicted at the beginning of your trip. This compares to a supervisor who is organized, and has good project management skills to keep the team and projects on track, while meeting deadlines.

The GPS also has the great feature of telling you ahead of time where you need to turn, stop, and merge. However, if you make a mistake and miss your turn, the GPS reroutes you to get you back on track. This compares to a leader or supervisor who looks at failures as opportunities to redirect the team. He or she understands that failure is finding out early that what you are currently doing is not right and the answer is still to be found. This type of leader encourages the team to keep going without judgement of incompetence.

Finally, when the GPS tells you that you have arrived at your destination and completed your journey, there is always a sense of accomplishment and gratitude for arriving safely to your destination. This compares to the leader who communicates that the projects are complete and celebrates with the team! The employees feel engagement and their morale increases, which results in job satisfaction and retention.

Supervisors, do be aware of micromanaging! Micromanaging is like being the backseat driver… making comments about how to drive every step of the journey, despite having given employees the tasks to complete their duties. This type of managing destroys communication and creativity, as well as the employee's engagement and morale. Micromanaging behaviors by a supervisor is one of the main reasons that employees leave their jobs.

Avoid being a backseat driver. Instead, empower and trust your team members. Support them, guide them, and let them drive. Use the GPS leadership example to lead your teams and accelerate team performance and job satisfaction! The employees will learn to be independent and creative, and they will help you get to the destination to meet your company's strategic goals.

The GPS is a great communication device that consistently guides you the entire time to your final destination, like a leader who creates a high-trust culture of accountability in the workplace. This is accountability and trust at its best!

"Employees buy-in to the leader first… then to their jobs and the organization."

~ Bella Cruz

Principle 6
Communicate Clear
Project Expectations

The Dos

1) DO communicate clearly

Many supervisors and teams don't have open communication, so they wind up working alone. The supervisor is busy with his or her work, and the team is too. They go days and weeks without updating each other. They are focusing on their personal priorities separately. Effective, continuous communication is important in order to close this gap.

Effective communication is all about listening to and understanding other people's point of view. What are they thinking? What inspires and motivates them? What challenges are they facing? Each employee has different skills to contribute to the team. The journey that you take to find out who they are and how you can help them is richly rewarding, both personally and professionally.

Communication is an essential life skill. It takes effort and energy because you have to think and concentrate on others and, at the same time, make them feel like they matter. You will gain your employees' loyalty, trust, and respect when you communicate with sincerity and take action with their success in mind.

2) DO explain the purpose of projects

It might surprise you how many departments work on projects that add no business value to the company. Lack of real purpose causes project failure.

"Consider the following statistic: 9.9% of every dollar is wasted due to poor project performance, according to the Project Management Institute's

(PMI) 2018 Pulse of the Profession Report. That represents $99 million for every $1 billion invested."[30]

The purpose of a project becomes the roadmap that guides the team in the right direction from start to finish. Start creating the project's focus by asking:

1) Why is the project being implemented?
2) What are its benefits?
3) How does it align with your company's strategic goals?
4) How is the end result supposed to look?
5) Clearly communicate to your team what you expect success to look like so that they can focus on those results.

When the supervisor identifies the project's purpose and communicates it to the team with clarity, the team begins working towards a common goal. Its members become engaged, and engaged teams make your customers happy.

"The purpose of business is to create and keep a customer."

~ Peter Drucker

3) **DO communicate how an employee's job impacts the company**

So many supervisors assume that their employees know how their job contributes to the entire company. However, employees don't know how their job affects the company if the supervisor doesn't tell them. Communicate this information as soon as you hire someone. When an employee knows how his or her role and responsibilities impact the company; they feel significant, and they are inspired to perform to the best of their ability.

4) **DO explain the who, what, when, where, and how for projects**

Has someone ever told you that they couldn't read your mind because they didn't know what you were thinking? That is how your employees feel if you provide them with little or no information about a project.

Remember, if you don't fill in the blanks for your team when they have questions, someone else will! The unofficial leader may not know what to do either, and might even steer your team in the wrong direction… but these people are usually good communicators who make people feel like they matter.

Taking the time to answer the who, what, when, where, and how when assigning projects gives the team direction and answers many of their questions. This process will put hours back into your schedule. The team will always have questions, but as you move through the project, they will feel confident relying on your direction to accomplish it when you effectively communicate and answer their questions.

"If you don't fill in the blanks for your team when they have questions, someone else will!"
~ Bella Cruz

5) **DO** follow up on projects regularly

How many times has your team given you a project update, and it wasn't at all what you expected? It had to be discouraging for you, and it certainly was for your team. Add in all the salaries in the room and multiply them by the time it took them to work on the project, and you'll start to see how costly it is not to communicate clearly.

6) **DO give the team feedback during the project**

There is nothing more frustrating to an employee than getting no support from a supervisor during a project. It's even more frustrating when the supervisor waits until the very end of a project to ask about it, causing unnecessary rework because it's nothing like what the supervisor expected.

The team members want their supervisor to communicate during the project. Why? Because they want to make sure that they are on track in order to make modifications to the project as needed, that all their questions are answered, and that issues are resolved so that they can do a good job for you!

Put ongoing team meetings on everyone's calendar to discuss a project's progression. The project will only be as important to the team as it is to you, so if you don't show up for the meetings, they won't either. They may physically be in the meeting, but if they are not engaged, they might as well be absent!

The following are some questions you can ask the team to get feedback on a project to improve performance. Get ready to write down ideas and concerns, help remove barriers, and ask for recommendations because the team will have some for you!

More *Team Performance Questions*

1) What are our customers saying about us?
2) What is the one thing we can do right now to improve our services/product lines?
3) How can I make your job better?

The information you get from the employees is like a gold mine… The more you dig, the more information you will discover to help you grow and scale your business.

7) **DO use digital technology and project management tools to keep everyone focused**

Today, leaders who are not keeping up with technology are not considered innovative or competitive.

There are many digital technologies and project management tools available to help you keep the team focused and up-to-date on project details. Accountable leaders investigate these tools and others so that they can keep their team operating with efficiency and give their company a competitive edge.

It's also important to use the right tools for you and your company. One company told me that it bought a project management software program for the entire company. However, very few people in the organization used it because it was too complicated and time-consuming. It can become costly if companies buy software and training programs, etc., for the entire company before doing research, pilots, and surveys with the employees.

> "Leaders often focus more on the system changes rather than the people that have to make and live with them. Don't forget that while you need to have systems in place, it's the people who matter most."[31]

8) DO communicate when the project is completed

Many employees have shared with me in workshops that their supervisors don't tell them when projects are complete. Some teams find out that their projects are completed when the supervisor is accepting an award at a company meeting; others find out through coworkers in other departments; and some never know if the project was ever completed. Imagine how frustrating that must be!

Just because a team stops working on a project does not mean it was successfully completed. It's important for the supervisor to communicate when projects are done and to celebrate the team's success soon after the project is completed.

Leadership Questions

1) What do your speech, body language, and written words say to others when you are communicating with them? How do you make them feel?

_____

_____

_____

2) How do you know you are giving your team the instructions it needs to successfully complete a project?

_____

_____

_____

Principle 6
Communicate Clear
Project Expectations

The "No Instructions" Leader

Employees want supervisors to communicate clear instructions when they assign projects. When they don't, the team can feel like it's getting a package the size of a car in the mail. This compares to a work project. There are thousands of pieces inside the box — whatever is inside clearly needs assembly, but there are no instructions. This compares to the supervisor delegating the project without communicating the instructions or expectations. When the team tries to contact support for the instructions, it can't reach anyone. This compares to the supervisor who is unapproachable, does not communicate successfully with the team, or is chronically absent.

Does the team figure out how to complete the project? Some teams do, some teams don't, and some teams don't want to because they are so discouraged! It's devastating to morale and engagement. When the supervisor stops by to occasionally ask, "How are things going?" the employees say that everything is fine. Why? They don't want to look incompetent.

Remember, silence isn't golden when it comes to teamwork and projects. It means that something is wrong with the team, and you haven't made its members feel like they could tell you what is really going on with their projects and the customers. Not being available or not communicating with employees will make them take more time to finish projects because you can almost guarantee that there will be rework. And rework is costly!

Now let's look at a story of two individuals: medical clinic supervisor Karen Thomas and her employee, Sam Keller. Flu season was approaching in a matter of weeks, and patients would be flooding in for their flu shots. Karen was busy preparing her team and clinic for the expected heavy traffic. "Let's take inventory of our supplies and be sure to place an order soon. We'll need to order flu shots too."

"But ma'am," one of her employees advised, "that's usually Macie's job, and she's on leave. She won't be back until after the start of the flu season."

Karen nodded. "Ah, I see. Sam, you go ahead and order supplies for us this week."

Her request caught him off guard. He didn't know how to order supplies. It wasn't something his job description needed him to know. But after a moment of hesitation, he agreed. *I'll figure it out,* he thought to himself.

Karen gave him the thumbs-up. "Excellent." After their huddle, she sent Sam a follow-up email: "Sam, just to confirm, you are ordering our supplies for the flu season?"

Sam wanted to take the opportunity to ask how to order supplies in the first place, but he felt conflicted and thought to himself: *I already agreed to do it; I can't ask how it's done. I don't want to look foolish.* So, he put it off, and put it off, and put it off. Karen, who was busy with her daily clinic operations, didn't notice and never followed up.

Before long, the day came. The first wave of flu shot patients entered the clinic for their appointments, expecting to be administered their shot as usual… but there were no vaccines available. Complaints began rolling in, and the patients were furious. They said: "Why are there no vaccines?" "Why didn't you call me to tell me there were no vaccines? I had to arrange my entire day for this appointment!" "Let me see your manager." "This is so unprofessional."

As the chorus of complaints rang out, patients with routine doctor's appointments couldn't help but to listen in. The whole waiting room was captivated by the flu shot train wreck. It was almost entertaining, until the lack of supplies interfered with their appointments too.

Then, the entire waiting room nearly became an angry mob. Even doctors began demanding an explanation.

When Karen found Sam, she was angry. She, too, demanded an explanation.

Sam answered, "I got busy and forgot."

"That's really all you've got to say for yourself? I can't believe this." She continued with questions until he finally told her that he didn't know how to order supplies.

"If you didn't know, why didn't you just ask?"

He wasn't about to admit the real reason. Sam just shrugged. "You didn't tell me how to order supplies. This is not my fault."

"46% of employees generally never know what they are supposed to do after leaving a meeting, according to Entrepreneur."[32]

For Karen, the difference between clear and unclear communication was pretty disastrous.

The following scenarios happened due to unclear communication:

1) Bad customer service/experience: patients were inconvenienced and left with a very negative impression of the clinic.
2) Blow to morale: customers' negative responses to the situation hurt the staff's team dynamics.
3) Stopped progress: employees from other departments had to stop their work to help with the angry patients.
4) Significant loss of revenue: the clinic lost revenue not only because of the appointments that were canceled, but also because of the resources that had to be diverted due to canceled appointments.
5) Bad PR: some patients posted about the incident on social media.

"Commonly cited statistics claim that human error is responsible for anywhere between 70-100% of incidents."[33]

When employees don't understand how they affect the grander operations of the company, they can cost their organization hundreds of thousands or even millions of dollars. Communicating clear expectations, knowing the employees' roles and responsibilities, providing training, and asking open-ended questions about every project can help prevent this kind of chaos.

Principle 6
Communicate Clear
Project Expectations

The Don'ts

1) DON'T ignore silence

If there is silence in the room, something is wrong. People are constantly communicating, even when they're not talking. People subconsciously express themselves with their facial expressions and body language; pay attention to the signals so that you can communicate better with others.

"While the key to success in both personal and professional relationships lies in your ability to communicate well, it's not the words that you use but your nonverbal cues or "body language" that speak the loudest."[34]

2) DON'T ask for a project status only when there are problems

"Leaders who ranked at the top 10% in asking for feedback were rated, on average, at the 86th percentile in overall leadership effectiveness. Feedback is also tied to employee engagement."[35]

Most of us have worked with a supervisors who only met with us when something went wrong. They usually say something like: "We need to talk," or "Can I see you in my office right away?" These words are terrifying to most people; their hearts start pounding, and their thoughts are racing. And if the supervisor can't meet with them right away, the focus shifts from their assigned tasks to "What did I do wrong?"

Supervisors, please don't keep employees wondering about what you need from them. Also, tell them what the meeting is about when you schedule it.

Believe me, they will worry about what's going to happen in your meeting with them if you don't!

Communicate often and discuss your projects regularly as a team, so that you can monitor and evaluate progress and ensure that they're on the right track. Not only does this create accountability, but you also get to explore ideas and receive feedback from your team during these ongoing meetings, which will encourage you to solve problems together.

3) DON'T ignore conflict

It is so uncomfortable for an employee to see conflict among the team go unacknowledged by its supervisor. Unresolved issues get bigger, and the team becomes dysfunctional. Team collaboration disappears; some employees take sides, and others go silent; work suffers, and when people get tired of it or just plain fed up, they start looking for another job. This means high turnover and low morale for the company. All of this affects your customers, service lines, deliveries, and profits.

Supervisors can mitigate conflict by outlining what accountability standards look like in their workplace.

Leadership Questions

1) Which questions do you ask your team members to make sure that they understand what to do when you are assigning or following up on projects?

_____

_____

_____

2) How do you deal with conflict within the team?

_____

_____

_____

Principle 7
Accept Accountability When the Team Fails — No Excuses!

The "Accountability Service" Leader

I had the great privilege of working with the U.S. Department of Defense for twelve years as a civilian. Due to rotating assignments, I saw a lot of leaders come and go. The military was like any other organization in its variety of leadership styles with civilians as well as military staff; some led well, and others needed coaching. But among them all, one leader stood out for his unmatched dedication to his people. His name was Colonel James Thor.

When Colonel Thor retired from his military service, he had one of the grandest receptions I had ever seen. I've been to retirement celebrations for leaders whose entire families lived in the same town and didn't attend the ceremony. But for Colonel Thor, even childhood friends flew in from out-of-town to congratulate him. His ceremony was held outside in a huge courtyard overflowing with executives, employees, parents, family, and friends.

At the front of the crowd stood Colonel Thor's team, who had dutifully supported him. During the party, they fondly recounted the time that he helped them prepare for a compliance inspection. They were all hands-on deck, but someone of Thor's rank was not expected to help, especially not with the cleaning. When he joined his team in scrubbing the cabinets, they rushed to stop him: "Sir, you don't have to do that. We'll take care of it!" He just smiled and said, "We're together in war; we're together in everything we do." Everyone was inspired, and no one forgot his support. When it came to accountability, you could count on him to courageously stand with his teams and be the first to take responsibility!

Behind Colonel Thor's teams were dozens of other department members whose lives he had personally touched. Many of them he had called or visited while they were in the hospital; he attended company barbecues, office holiday celebrations, and employee award ceremonies over the years. When the office potluck dish sign-up list made its rounds to celebrate holidays, meat — the most expensive dish — was always the last thing anyone signed up to bring. But Colonel Thor had that item taken off the list and took care of it himself. You may be thinking, "Why would you mention a potluck?" Because everyone noticed. If necessary, he would also pay out of pocket to replace department appliances. If you had used the employee microwave or refrigerator, you could thank Colonel Thor for providing it. He never told anyone that he did these things, but everyone knew.

It was an emotional celebration, and many couldn't hold back tears, including me. I had been through a lot with Colonel Thor over his time at that military base. In one deeply moving display of honor, I saw him provide several arrangements of memorial flowers for a soldier's wife when he noticed that there were none at the funeral. Later, we found out that the soldier had no family except for his wife.

Competence is crucial to leadership, and Colonel Thor was certainly a leader with integrity and competence. He produced exemplary results in the business and military operations for which he was responsible. Undoubtedly, this was due to his accountability, his *service* to his teams and his department, and their trust in him. Accountability is not just showing up; it's also how you provide *service* to your teams. Every chance he got, he showed them that he cared for them, and in return, they became the most loyal outfit I had ever seen. It has been years since I worked with Colonel James Thor, but how he made us feel and the service he gave to us will always come to mind when I think of excellent and influential servant leadership.

"When people see you or hear your name 20 or 30 years from now, they won't remember the projects you worked on, or the awards you won. They will remember how you made them feel!"

~ Bella Cruz

Principle 7
Accept Accountability When the Team Fails — No Excuses!

The Dos

1) DO hold yourself accountable

Leaders lead by example. When you hold yourself accountable, you communicate that accountability is a priority, and you encourage the same from your employees. When everyone is accountable, you've created a high-trust culture of accountability in your workplace. And once you've done that, you've proven yourself reliable to your team. They know that they can trust you to get things done, to advocate for them, to act in their best interest, and to support them. And when they fail, they know that they can trust you to get them back on track without fear of retribution, and that you will support them and stand by them. This directly translates to a working environment based on loyalty, respect and, ultimately, increased customer satisfaction.

> "At the end of the day we are accountable to ourselves — our success is a result of what we do."
>
> ~ Catherine Pulsifer

2) DO hold the team accountable

So many supervisors have told me that it's difficult for them to hold people accountable. They say that they feel like they're initiating conflict, which they would rather not deal with. Some supervisors would rather be liked than lead, and some don't have the training or coaching skills to facilitate these types of conversations or scenarios.

Let's be clear: accountability and conflict are not the same thing. But even so, these kinds of supervisors are unwise to avoid conflict, which destroys morale and efficiency in the workplace. Getting the best performance from the team requires you to efficiently manage conflict, and addressing it sensibly improves team focus, autonomy, and job satisfaction. The proper training can help you develop your conflict resolution skills.

"Accountability breeds response-ability."

~ Stephen R. Covey

3) **DO include the entire team when being recognized**

How many times have you seen an award ceremony where an executive or supervisor gets a team award, and thanks everyone else in the room with an executive title but forgets to thank the team? Don't get me wrong; the executives should be and deserve to be acknowledged. But no matter what the award, the team members had a part to play in earning it, and they deserve their due recognition.

People work hard at their jobs, and most of their time during the week is spent at work. When someone gets an award, it should be celebrated with respect and honor, whether it's an individual or the entire team. When you celebrate their successes with them, employees lean in and engage. Some may perform better because of the recognition, but many others will lean in simply because they know that their effort isn't going unnoticed.

Reward your team as soon as it finishes a project. The award doesn't mean as much if you mention it months later. Don't forget to give your management team awards too; like everyone else, they want to get awards for a job well done! Inclusive recognition does wonders for morale. Some ideas for presenting awards are:

1) Announce the awards formally in a staff meeting or at a quarterly company event.
2) Make sure the person getting the award is present! I've seen and heard of many supervisors announcing awards without the recipient being present, or just putting an award on a desk without any mention of why he or she received it. When you are intentional about creating an appreciative atmosphere at the awards ceremony, the employee feels truly recognized.

3) Always explain why the person is being recognized. How did he or she contribute? What did he or she do well? Accomplish for the company?

4) Provide food at the event, if possible, to celebrate.

Employees work hard to earn their awards. They will become more engaged if you celebrate them with the respect and the honor they deserve for a job well done.

4) **DO** hire people that take accountability

It is important to hire people whose values align with your company's values. So, when you've established that you value accountability, it is important to hire accountable employees. Employees who take responsibility for their actions, keep their commitments, and own their mistakes in order to preserve your high-trust, accountable workplace culture.

Leadership Questions

1) How do you show accountability "service" to your team?

_____

_____

_____

2) What award criteria do you use to celebrate the team for a job well done?

_____

_____

_____

3) How do you present awards to your team?

_____

_____

_____

Principle 7
Accept Accountability When the Team Fails – No Excuses!

The "Pass The Buck" Leader

The room was quiet. A speaker stood at the front of a conference room delivering a presentation about what could be improved in her department. This government organization's senior executives had asked this team member and many others like her to identify problems in order to improve the organization. The teams would then present their findings as part of the same agenda that I had been brought in to facilitate.

This speaker was not the first to present that day, nor was she the last. She didn't say anything particularly controversial, she didn't use inflammatory language, and she wasn't disrespectful in any way. And yet, her presentation was easily the most memorable because of her supervisor!

While the speaker was making her presentation on the department's current issues, the supervisor stood up and began bombarding the attendees with excuses like: "We've been having turnover; we're short-staffed; the manager is new, and he's still learning the job; our work has been delayed by other departments." She rattled off the list so effortlessly that it seemed as if she had been rehearsing it in her mind.

After about 30 seconds of blame-throwing, one of the executives finally interrupted her and said, "Your team is doing a great job and did what we asked them to do. We are looking forward to its next presentation." Embarrassed, the supervisor sheepishly sat back down. The result was that she took absolutely no accountability as a leader, and she openly blamed the team in front of the entire organization for areas that needed improvement in her department.

Once the presentations were finished, this supervisor's team rushed out of the room and avoided her gaze. They were beyond discouraged, and you could see it on their faces. Unsurprisingly, she had singlehandedly demolished not only her team's morale, but also their trust in and respect for her as their leader. Now the organization also knew about this manager's lack of accountability. And at the end of this project, this team had produced minimal results

Supporting your team members and standing by them through success and failure alike is foundational to gaining their trust and respecting you as their leader.

"Everything rises and falls on leadership."
~ John Maxwell

Lack of Accountability & Trust in the Workplace

Lack of accountability and trust by the leader or supervisor can remove focus from the business's strategic goals and impact the team. Employees can become disengaged and, ultimately, this creates a low trust workplace culture that can cost organizations billions of dollars every year.

> "According to Gallup, disengaged employees have 37% higher absenteeism, 18% lower productivity, and 15% lower profitability. When that translates into dollars, you're looking at the cost of 34% of a disengaged employee's annual salary, or $3,400 for every $10,000 they make."[36]

Lack of Accountability from Disengaged Employees

The following are some examples of lack of accountability behaviors in the workplace that can be costly for the organization.

1) Employees telling customers, "That's not my department," or "It's not my job," when they ask for help.

2) Employees telling customers, "I'm on a break," when they ask for help.

3) Employees complaining that they don't get promoted, but they don't take the initiative to learn anything new outside their current job description to help others and the company.

4) Employees having personal conversations or eating in front of customers.

5) Employees scrolling through their phone or texting while working, especially in front of the customers.

6) Employees being familiar with company product lines and policies, but not sharing the information with customers.

7) Employees not observing proper hygiene protocols (i.e., not washing hands after using the facilities etc.).

8) Employees transferring customers to another department on the phone without explanation. This is called a blind transfer, and these transfers are extremely frustrating for the customer because he or she has to explain the problem all over again to the next agent.

9) Employees not acknowledging customers when they walk into the store or business.

10) Employees walking the other way when they see customers with the "I'm lost" look on their faces.

11) Employees being rude to customers in person, on the phone, or via digital technology.

12) Calling in at the last minute or showing up late to work consistently.

Lack of Accountability Between Disengaged Co-workers

1) Employees not reporting broken equipment or necessary repairs. This results in longer wait times for employees and customers.

2) Employees not returning phone calls or emails on time, or at all.

3) Employees not meeting project deadlines or asking for help when they need it.

4) Employees removing their personal protective equipment (PPE) or failing to comply with safety policies unless they are being audited or the supervisor is nearby.

5) Employees stealing company supplies.

6) Employees talking negatively about co-workers, supervisors, or the organization to customers or coworkers, etc.

7) Employees gossiping and creating cliques within the department that create division between team members.

8) Employees failing to contribute any new ideas, or solve problems to help others.

9) Employees turning off video view during virtual meetings and doing other things instead of engaging with the team.

Principle 7
Accept Accountability When the Team Fails — No Excuses!

The Don'ts

1) DON'T blame the team for failures and mistakes

"A CEO said… "Yesterday I got furious with one of my senior leaders because of a mistake he made. I ripped into him during our senior leadership meeting. I was so convinced that the problem we were having was all his fault. And then I was sitting at my home computer when I received a notification from LinkedIn that Bob had just updated his profile, and my heart sank as I realized he might be about to quit."[37]

Yes, each of us is personally responsible for our own actions. But who is responsible for leading the team? A leader who blames others is saying, "It's not my fault!" This kind of mindset is the total opposite of accountability. It models blame-throwing and destroys morale in the workplace.

Good leaders take accountability seriously and own their mistakes. They reframe failure and mistakes as opportunities to reinvent and get back on the right track. They are grateful for finding out sooner than later that they were on the wrong track, and that the failure was a sign to keep searching for the answers that are still ahead to produce a successful team project.

2) DON'T blame your boss

People who blame others might also blame their own supervisors when they don't want to take responsibility for what happens in the workplace.

"The reality is you set the tone by how you behave and act, so if you want an underperforming organization, just allow passing the buck to be the norm.

The Bottom Line: Passing the buck is never a good strategy when it comes to being a successful leader."[38]

When you acknowledge your role in failure and take the opportunity to adjust, you are not only modeling healthy workplace behaviors… you are sustaining a high-trust accountability culture… you are earning the support, loyalty, and respect of your team.

Leadership Questions

1) How do you handle mistakes when the team fails?

_____

_____

_____

2) How do you support your team in front of others when they fail?

_____

_____

_____

Conclusion

In my 25-year career as an executive coach, leadership strategist, and motivational global speaker, the two areas where companies needed the most help — and that were most vital to their success — were, and are, trust and accountability.

Trust and accountability… two ideas that, on the surface, seem so simple. We hear these words every day in hundreds of different contexts. It is easy to believe that we know what they mean and how they look.

But when you look more closely, trust and accountability show their true natures: multifaceted, nuanced, and complex. What does it mean to be trustworthy *in this situation?* How do leaders earnestly convey their trustworthiness *day to day?* How do leaders hold themselves accountable *right now?* How do they use their tone of voice, their facial expressions, and their body language to hold a team member accountable respectfully? Sensitively? Fairly?

These are some of the important questions all leaders must answer in their specific situation, and the pursuit of their answers is a courageous one. Your team is relying on that courageous pursuit.

Leaders and supervisors are the pulse of any organization. If the pulse is strong, the organization is strong; if it is weak, the organization is weak. There are leaders who earn their employees' trust, hold themselves accountable, and model these behaviors for their employees to flourish, and there are leaders who don't.

If you are reading these words, I commend your commitment to your team. Reading this book represents an important first step toward transforming your workplace into a high-trust culture of accountability. Why else would someone read a book titled *Please Fire Me! I Can't Stand My Boss (How Today's Leaders Build Relationships, Job Satisfaction, & Retention)?*

The principles in this book have been proven to improve turnover rate, engagement, efficiency, customer satisfaction and, yes, the bottom line. If you apply them consistently, you will notice a dramatic change in your department and organization.

But if you want to take the next step, if you want to see the full potential of what practical trust and accountability can do for *your* team and *your* organization, my team and I are here to help.

Visit: www.Created2Lead.com

Author Biography

Bella Cruz, M.A., is an Amazon #1 international bestselling author, an award-winning global motivational speaker, executive coach, corporate strategist, and philanthropist.

Bella is an expert in developing leaders, engaging teams, and igniting growth.

She is a certified Six Sigma Black Belt, earned a master's degree, and has more than 25 years' experience in the corporate world.

Before launching her career, Bella navigated homelessness as a single mother and now gives a portion of all her book sales to support her local food bank as one of her charities.

She lives in Texas where she enjoys family time, barbeques, and the outdoors.

BUILDING LEADERS | BUILDING LEGACIES®

Created 2 Lead Services

Motivational Keynotes

Conferences, Women's Conferences, Events, Retreats & Seminars

Executive & Leadership Coaching

One-on-One or Team Coaching

Leadership & Employee Training

Workshops & Masterminds

Visit

www.created2lead.com

Today!

Join Bella in her book *Created 2 Lead 4 Kids,*
Making Chores Fun
for a quick, fun tale where she learns...

Leadership Skills |Taking Initiative |Teamwork
and Creative Problem Solving while having fun!

IGNITE THE LEADER WITHIN YOU
with Bella Cruz's
Bestselling Leadership Quotes

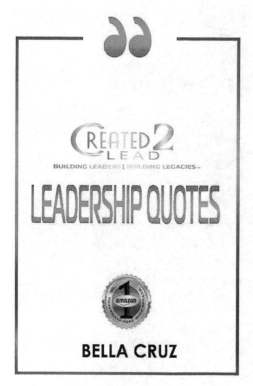

Created 2 Lead Leadership Quotes are taken from the book *Please Fire Me! I Can't Stand My Boss (How Today's Leaders Build Relationships, Job Satisfaction & Retention)* by Bella Cruz.

Use the *Created 2 Lead Leadership Quotes* to help you create a high-trust culture of accountability in the workplace.

The book contains questions to help you assess your leadership style to inspire and motivate you to connect with your team(s) to enhance relationships, boost engagement, morale, and accelerate team performance for greater levels of productivity.

CREATE 2 LEAD
LEADERSHIP QUOTES

Notes

1. Quain, S. (2019, Feb 01). Chron. Retrieved from Why is Honesty Important to Business? Small Business, Business communications & Etiquette, Importance of Business Communication.

2. Ward, G. (2018, November 12). 7 Practices That Will Make You A Respectful Leader. Retrieved from Greggwardgroup.

3. Quy, L. (2019, March 22). Ladders Fast On Your Feet, This is the best way to detect a lack of integrity in others. Retrieved from Ladders Fast On Your Feet.

4. psi, testing excellence. (2013, November 06). Retrieved from There is No Shortcut to Safety.

5. Benstead, S. (2018, July 13). Top reasons employees don't trust their managers revealed.

6. Wax, D. (n.d.). "Writing and Remembering: Why We Remember What We Write." Retrieved from "Writing and Remembering: Why We Remember What We Write."

7. Trustworthy. (2020, December 1). The Deboer Fellowship, How to Spot an Incompetent Leader. Retrieved from Harvard Business Review.

8. Klas, T. (2020, February 24). Training Industry, Leadership 6 Steps to Becoming an Approachable Leader.

9. (Team, Mind Tools, How approachable Are you? Building Relationships With Your Team)

10. Hamer, L. (n.d.). The Muse, Networking, The Secret to Being Approachable is Almost Too Obvious (You've Probably Already Done it Today).

11. (Benstead, op reasons employee don't trust their managers revealed, 2018)

12. Anderson, B. (2019, May 16). Onboarding, What is the Cost of Onboarding and employee [Calculator].

13. llan Lee, S. W. (2018, March 02). Harvard Business Review. Motivating People, When Empowering Employees Works, and When It doesn't.

14. Human Resources, E. L. (2018, March 07). OSU.EDU, Playing Favorites: A Study of Perceived Workplace Favoritism.

15. Team, I. E. (2021, February 26). 35 Behavioral Interview Questions.

16. Brent Gleeson, A. G. (n.d.). Insomnia Escape Room DC from article Forbes, 10 unique perspectives On what makes a great leader.

17. Porath, C. (2015). Harvard Business Review. The Leadership Behavior That's Most Important to Employees.

18. OSU.edu. (2018, March 07). Lead Read Today, Playing Favorites: A Study of Perceived Workplace Favoritism.

19. OSU.edu. (2018, March 07). Playing Favorites: A Study of Perceived Workplace Favoritism.

20. In my 25-year coaching and speaking career, I have seen employees seek legal retribution against their companies for favoritism. But I am not a lawyer, and I am not giving legal advice. I am only making you aware of the potential consequences of favoritism. Speak with your company's HR department to learn their specific policies and develop a plan of action to prevent favoritism in the workplace.

21. IQ, D. (2018, November 20). The effects of favoritism are detrimental in the dental workplace.

22. Bowser, J. (2019, April 18). Holding employees accountable: where most leaders fail. LinkedIn articles.

23. Evans, C. (2020, December 30). The 5 things No One Told You About Accountability in Leadership,' Eagle's Flight.

24. Ryan, K. (n.d.). Pinnacle Coaching Group. Retrieved from Leadership Toolbox: Don't Be Afraid to Take Action.

25. Zak, P. J. (2019, February). Harvard Business Review. Retrieved from The Neuroscience of Trust, Management behaviors that foster employee engagement.

26. Group, S. I. (2017, August 14). The Steps to Minimizing Costly Employee Errors.

27. Yatcilla, C. (2019, March 08). PRIMEPAY article. Retrieved from POSTED IN HUMAN RESOURCES.

28. Institute, P. M. (2018). Pulse of the Profession. Retrieved from Success Disruptive Times, Expanding the Value Delivery Landscape to Address the High Cost of Low Performance.

29. Experts, P. (2019, August 30). 11 Tips for Effective Employee Communication. Retrieved from Primepay Blog.

30. NOPSEMA. (n.d.). Australia's Offshore energy regulator, Human Factors.

31. HelpGuide. (n.d.). Nonverbal Communication and Body Language.

32. Craven, J. (2016, July 16). Forbes. Retrieved from Being A Great Leader Means Giving and Receiving Feedback.

33. Borysenko, K. (2019, May 02). How Much Are Your Disengaged Employees Costing you?

34. Wilikie, D. (2017, August 29). SHRM Better Workplaces Better World, Your Employee Messes Up: How Do You Respond? Dos & Don'ts for addressing workers mistakes.

35. Achievements, G. a. (n.d.). The Consequences of Passing The Buck As a Leader, Goals and Achievements.

36. Arabian Business, People will continue to leave their jobs because of their managers, Justin McGuire, co-founder & CEO — MENA & APAC of DMCG Global, tackles an uncomfortable truth for companies, Dec 1, 2020.

37. The Consequences of Passing the Buck as a Leader, Goals and Achievements, https://www.goalsandachievements.co.uk/blog/the-consequences-of-passing-the-buck-as-a-leader/